Anat Garti, Shay Tzafrir
Work–Family Triangle Synchronization

Anat Garti, Shay Tzafrir

Work–Family Triangle Synchronization

Employee, manager, and spouse

DE GRUYTER

ISBN 978-3-11-153011-6
e-ISBN (PDF) 978-3-11-075980-8
e-ISBN (EPUB) 978-3-11-075998-3

Library of Congress Control Number: 2022938160

Bibliographic information published by the Deutsche Nationalbibliothek
The Deutsche Nationalbibliothek lists this publication in the Deutsche
Nationalbibliografie; detailed bibliographic data are available on the internet at http://
dnb.dnb.de.

www.degruyter.com

Acknowledgments

We are deeply thankful for the assistance of many readers and colleagues along the way. We personally wish to thank the managers, employees, and spouses we interviewed over the years for giving us a deep view into their work–family challenges.

A special thanks to our families. This book would not have been possible without the support of our spouses, Dror and Dalit, our parents—Leonore and Shlomo; and Zwi and Nitza—and our children—Rotem, Amit, and Noa; and Itay and Rotem. We thank them for the helpful suggestions we received and for their interest, patience, and guidance.

https://doi.org/10.1515/9783110759808-202

Contents

Introduction

The world we knew before the pandemic (COVID-19) will not be the same world after it ends. The pandemic created a global transformation in many spheres, including family, work, employment, organizations, and the economy. Our reaction to this disruption should involve stopping for a moment and examining its effects in depth and our future strategies, actions, and practices. This analysis needs to be done both separately in many social spheres and in an integrative way that incorporates those spheres. It is clear to all of us that the world of work has changed radically, and a wider space has been created for remote work, mutual jobs, hybrid work, agility, new performance evaluations, communication, new business models, and the nature of leadership. As technology adoption and acceptance increases, it has had a rapid and significant effect on employment patterns. The digital age, also called the information age, in which personal computers with the ability to transfer information freely and quickly were introduced, is already far behind us. The virtual age now allows an individual with computerized glasses to create an avatar and experience, play, and work in formed environments and interact with other avatars. The reality in which technology is, almost for everyone, everywhere and available at all times leads to the amalgamation of people, virtual worlds, and machines, leading to employment clarifications and possibilities, sometimes beyond imagination, including the creation of collective intelligence.

Technology today allows small organizations (not only multinational corporations) to look for talent anywhere around the globe, turning the labor market into a small village. The fact that availability no longer has to be physical, we have to modify our expectations about our organization. Office is no longer a static place we visit, but it can be a virtual place that we can access at any given moment from any place. The entry of younger generations into the labor market accustomed to virtual environments has led to thinking about how work takes place and what type of workers we desire. Yet at the same time, it is clear to everyone that we remain social "animals" with a need for nourishing social interactions in general and in our working environment. The human factor emphasizing human capital (knowledge, skills, and abilities, or KSA) has become more significant, despite the widespread entry of artificial intelligence because of its capabilities to upgrade organizational performance in the organizational managerial "jungle." Thus, the availability and KSA qualities of individuals, trust, and belonging have become key aspects in organizational interactions, certainly among individuals defined as organizational talents.

Individuals, families, and organizations ask themselves: How will those transformations affect us as individuals, a family, a group, and an organization in various aspects such as work and the society in which live? What will be our working time? These questions dismantle and reassemble the basic assumptions of the world of work and put more focus on the assumption of heterogeneity between organizations and individuals operating in them, as this becomes a more multifaceted and multidi-

https://doi.org/10.1515/9783110759808-204

mensional world. Facing diverse employees alongside organizations that offer various jobs and tasks creates a huge challenge for managers. Thus, organizations and companies look for KSA such as science, technology, engineering, or mathematics, even in non-technological professions, along with flexibility, adaptation to change, task prioritization, parallel work, virtual teamwork, effective communication, and analytic ability. In addition, individuals are required to work alongside machines and robots, and often do so in a virtual environment with their unique avatar.

Along with all these organizational transformations, our family sphere has faced many changes, too. Changes in marriage and childbearing have reshaped family structures during the past half-century. The age of marriage has risen; people are getting married later in life, and others are forgoing marriage altogether. The rise in the number of unmarried people, in turn, has contributed to an increasing share of births outside of marriage and children living with an unmarried parent. On average, families are smaller now, due to both the growth of single-parent households and the drop in fertility. Moreover, the circumstances surrounding parenthood have changed. Social changes toward gender equality and perceptions of fathers' roles occurred. At the same time, the role of mothers has changed, and more mothers have entered the labor force and become breadwinners—in some cases, the primary breadwinners—in their families.

The interface between these two worlds that began many years ago as work–family conflict has been followed by the insight that this interface can also enrich the family (work–family enrichment), thus creating a new challenge. Is it possible to rely on past precedent and predict what will happen in the future? The answer, in our opinion, is more complex than yes or no. This situation involves another turning point, given the massive changes in remote work (work from home), exponential advances in technology, and changes in people's value system. Researchers, consultants, CEOs, and other professionals looked at four basic levels of analysis—individual, group, organization, and country—to analyze and understand what happened and where to proceed. Building on these levels, we suggest focusing on the interface between organizations and families and the daily interactions between three people—manager, employee and spouse. This is the triangle that manages daily work and family interactions. In many cases we have to consider four people (the couple and their managers). This conclusion is due to the fact that social values and lifestyle have led many families to the conclusion that both spouses should work; therefore, the number of families in which both spouses are working has increased dramatically. It is important to note that throughout the book, we refer to couples as a man and woman. However, everything said in the book is also true for same-sex couples. Also, divorced couples (heterosexual or same sex) still manage in a certain way the work–family interface and therefore, everything written in this book is also true for them, with necessary adjustments depending on the nature of their divorce.

What happens in a situation where both spouses work and are repeatedly exposed to numerous demands and the levels of stress frequently become higher? Many organizations sincerely try, in a diverse world, to create inclusive work environments that provide all employees with a sense of belonging and a perception of equal opportunity for success. The first step in creating a more egalitarian workplace is understanding where and how the gaps between individuals in the organization begin to emerge. Understanding the situation in which people operate is essential and therefore, collecting data about individuals in the organization along their career path and social interactions is important and requires an understanding of what is happening to them at home. Consider a family in which both spouses work and have two school-age children. Try to imagine how that family starts the morning when all four individuals need to connect remotely with school and work. How do they get along? How should they act to be part of the family and part of their work at the same time? This is what our book is all about: how to cope with and accomplish all requirements and demands.

This book is based on the authors' academic research and field experience in the organizational and family domains for almost 20 years. It is an extension and update of research and practice in the field of work and family, with a distinct, innovative, and important framework. The book introduces a model, methodology, and compelling tools, accompanying the reader step by step in the task of developing a synchronized work–family triangle psychological contract, as both a diagnostic and management tool. It addresses human resource managers, organizational consultants, and couple therapists who face work–family challenges. Highlighting vignettes in the form of personal anecdotes and stories and including plenty of no-nonsense practical exercises, the book satisfies readers from all walks of working life, including managers, employees, and employees' spouses, who experience these work–family triangle interactions and are interested in helping themselves in managing their respective work–family conflict.

Chapter 1 introduces the reader to the work and family fields in this world of volatility, uncertainty, complexity, and ambiguity. It elaborates on frameworks of work–family conflict, work–family enrichment, and work–family balance. The purpose is to orient the reader with the varied updated literatures before we outline our groundbreaking approach to the interface: work–family triangle synchronization, or WFTS.

Chapter 2 elaborates on the work and family challenge at three levels—organization, team and individual—concluding that three stakeholders manage the daily interface: (a) manager, (b) employee, and (c) employee's spouse. These three are best represented in a triangle relationship that has to manage the work–family interface at the organization and team levels. In a dual-earner family, the system is composed of four stakeholders and their different, and sometimes conflicting, interests: (a) woman, (b) man, (c) woman's manager, and (d) man's manager.

Chapter 3 focuses on the psychological contract of each dyad relationship in the work–family triangle system: (a) manager–employee, (b) manager–employee's spouse, (c) couple relationship (employee–employee's spouse), and (d) woman's manager and man's manager. The chapter spotlights the indirect relationship between the manager and the employee's spouse due to its important impact on the other relationships in the triangles system.

Chapter 4 introduces the reader to the therapy triangle framework and then uses it to analyze the triad work–family relationship. Triangling occurs when the inevitable anxiety in a dyad is relieved by involving a vulnerable third party, who either takes sides or provides a detour for the anxiety. This creates movement in the triangle dyads. The chapter elaborates on the different movements of the work–family triangle system.

Chapter 5 explores the process in which the four stakeholders fulfill their work and family needs by utilizing work and family abilities, resulting in work and family well-being. Because the needs are sometimes in conflict, the triangle's relationship power has a significant effect on resolving the conflict. The chapter elaborates on the different ways a triangle can resolve conflicts, concluding that the best way is co-opetition, a clever cooperative use of the members' abilities to resolve the conflict brought on by competition. This is the WFTS process we suggest, ending in a triangle psychological contract.

Chapter 6 uses Dolan's triaxial model for the methodologic development of a triangle psychological contract. WFTS, constructed on the economic, ethical, and emotional axes of the triaxial model, promotes the development of a holistic psychological contract that addresses all needs and abilities of the triangle. The chapter introduces the reader to the triaxial model and then, step by step, accompanies the reader in the task of designing an appropriate and suitable work–family triangle psychological contract. This psychological contract should be tailored for the right people at the right time in the right context.

Chapter 7 presents the trust in work–family triangles. Trust as glue in any social relationship helps the triangle manage the triad relationship. The chapter presents Tzafrir and Dolan's trust-ME model based on reliability, concern, and harmony dimensions and accompanies the reader in building and developing a trust triangle relationship that will enable the fulfillment of the WFTS psychological contract.

Chapter 1
Work–Family Interface: An Overview

> Never get so busy making a living that you forget to make a life.
> – Dolly Parton, singer

For many years, the work–family interface was conceptualized as a conflict (e.g., Allen et al., 2013; Carlson et al., 2000; Ernst Kossek & Ozeki, 1998; Frone et al., 1992; Kossek et al., 2011; Moen et al., 2015; Netemeyer et al., 1996). In 1985, Greenhaus and Beutell defined work–family conflict as:

> A form of inter role conflict in which the role pressures from the work and family domains are mutually incompatible in some respect. That is, participation in the work (family) role is made more difficult by virtue of participation in the family (work) role. (p. 77)

This conceptualization is based primarily on role theory and the scarcity of resources hypothesis, which suggest that the demands of one role deplete personal resources, such as time and physical or mental energy, leaving insufficient resources to allocate to other roles (Edwards & Rothbard, 2000; Goode, 1960; Marks, 1977). Work–family conflict is associated with negative emotions and poor health (Allen & Armstrong, 2006; Greenhaus et al., 2006; Grzywacz, 2000; Grzywacz & Bass, 2003); different work outcomes, such as job stressors, job involvement, job dissatisfaction, job burnout, and turnover (Frone et al., 1992; Pleck et al., 1980); and psychological distress and life stress (Frone et al., 1992; Greenhaus & Beutell, 1985; Kluwer et al., 1996).

This framework of the work–family interface as separate conflicting spheres sets up a false dichotomy that fails to acknowledge that work is a part of life. This dichotomous approach to work and family issues results in an assumed adversarial relationship between work and family, which effectively perpetuates the stereotype of the ideal worker as one who not only places a firm boundary between the two but is also able and willing to put the work sphere ahead of the family sphere (Bruce & Reed, 1994).

For years, however, work–family conflict was the main work–family interface framework. The results of many studies have challenged this view of two separate, adversarial, zero-sum spheres, and researchers have established the goal of reconnecting them for the benefit of both individuals and the companies in which they work (Fletcher & Bailyn, 1996; Greenhaus & Powell, 2006; Halpern & Murphy, 2013; Kalliath, 2014; Rantanen et al., 2013). New conceptualizations, emphasizing the benefits of participating in both roles and the strong connection between the roles, were developed. Work–family enrichment (Greenhaus & Powell, 2006; Kalliath, 2014), reconnecting work and family (Fletcher & Bailyn, 1996), work–family interaction (Halpern & Murphy, 2013), and integrating work and family life (Bailyn et al., 2001; Parasuraman & Greenhaus, 1999) are some examples.

https://doi.org/10.1515/9783110759808-001

The nonconflict conceptualization that is widespread in the work and family field is that of work–family enrichment. The fundamental thinking underpinning work–family enrichment is that participation in multiple roles provides individuals with resources, such as self-esteem, self-confidence, knowledge, and skills, which can be used to benefit participation in other life domains (Kalliath, 2014). Work–family enrichment is defined as "the extent to which experiences in one role improve the quality of life in another role" (Greenhaus & Powell, 2006, p. 72).

Enrichment represents synergies that occur when the resources gained from participation in role A (at work or in the family) are used to enhance performance in role B (Greenhaus & Powell, 2006). For example, a social worker may learn mediation or conflict resolution skills at work, which may then be used effectively in a family situation. Similarly, effective parenting or multitasking skills acquired at home may be used effectively in a social work situation.

Greenhaus and Powell (2006) identified five types of resources that can be generated as a result of participation in a given role: (a) skills and perspectives (e.g., multitasking, interpersonal skills, respect for individual differences, and trust); (b) psychological and physical resources (e.g., self-esteem, positive emotions such as optimism, and physical health); (c) social capital (e.g., information and influence); (d) flexibility (e.g., time, space, and location for meeting the requirements of the role); and (e) material resources (e.g., money and gifts obtained from work and family).

The pathways by which these resources spill over and influence other roles include the instrumental path – that is, when the resources gained in one role (e.g., knowledge, skills, perspectives) may directly improve performance in another role – and the affective path, when resources gained from participation in one role (e.g., positive emotions) may indirectly improve performance in another role by virtue of influencing a positive affect (Greenhaus & Powell, 2006; Kalliath, 2014).

In the affective path, Greenhaus and Powell (2006) identified three ways in which participation in work and family roles can influence positive outcomes for individuals. First, experiences in work and family roles can have additive effects on individual well-being. Empirical evidence suggests that satisfied participation in multiple roles at work and in the family is associated with greater well-being (Barnett & Hyde, 2001; Perry-Jenkins et al., 2000). Second, participation in work and family roles can buffer the negative experiences of strain emanating from another role (Barnett et al., 1992). Third, experiences in one role (work or family) can create positive energies and affect, which can be used to enhance experiences in other roles (Marks, 1977; Sieber, 1974).

The work and family spheres simultaneously have an enrichment interface and a conflict interface. The idea of competitors working together to open new markets, develop new products, or improve the market position of all parties involved is termed in the business world "co-opetition" (cooperation combined with competition). The book *Co-opetition*, by Brandenburger and Nalebuff (1996), introduced the concept to the business world. The work–family triangle synchronization model presented in this book argues that although the resources, such as time and attention, of the work and family spheres are competitive, the spheres benefit from working together, including managing competitive resources together, and therefore, should learn to collaborate through co-opetition.

An important aspect of co-opetition is crossing boundaries. The centerpiece of this approach is a recognition of the added value that comes from permeating barriers that are traditionally perceived as fostering competition rather than cooperation, such as those among marketing, engineering, and research and development; barriers with external suppliers; and even competitive barriers between companies in the same industry (Ring & Van de Ven, 1994). Despite this new respect for crossing boundaries and co-opetition in the business world, the boundary between work and family remains "off limits" (Fletcher & Bailyn, 1996). In their book *Challenging the Last Boundary: Reconnecting Work and Family*, Fletcher and Bailyn (1996) described this paradox. Boundaryless organizations are populated by workers who have the skills to capture the synergy in crossing functional and occupational boundaries, but who nonetheless feel the need to maintain a strict separation between work and family. This sense of competing adversarial spheres runs so deep that even when crossing boundaries is listed as one of the meanings of a boundaryless career (Arthur, 1994), the two spheres are frequently cast as oppositional.

The COVID-19 pandemic challenged the boundaries between work and family like never before. One significant cross-boundary phenomenon is work from home (WFH). WFH emerged in the early 2000s, when telecommuting technologies started to develop and workers could WFH to avoid traveling, provide flexibility in schedules, and achieve a better work–life balance (Tavares, 2017). During the COVID-19 pandemic, especially during quarantines, many workers were instructed to WFH full time, which redefined the conventional concept of WFH as typical only for certain types of work, on an occasional basis, or given unique employee circumstances (Bouziri et al., 2020; Xiao et al., 2021). Once the dam opened, there was no way back. Many workers today demand the right to WFH, at least on some days, forcing organizations to adapt, whether they liked it or not.

This book takes things one step further, mapping the obstacles to eliminating boundaries between work and family and exploring ways to cope with them to build a co-opetition system. Instead of looking at work and family as allies or enemies, frames that are in use in the work and family field (Greenhaus & Powell, 2006; Powell & Eddleston, 2013), this book perceives them as partners in a competitive built-in situation that can benefit from working together.

Another new reality that emerged from the pandemic, confronting organizations with previous perceptions, is the "Great Resignation." Given the adverse impact of employment loss on financial and psychological well-being, we would expect that workers would be motivated to return to their jobs and willing to put the work sphere ahead of the family sphere even further. Contrary to expectations, at least some employees are re-examining their job and career options instead. Explanations for the phenomenon are that the widespread uncertainty of COVID-19 led workers to place the family before work, to consider alternatives they would never thought of before the pandemic, or simply realize that their work conditions have been unacceptable (Jiskrova, 2022).

Managing the work–family interface through work–family triangle synchronization addresses this phenomenon as well. Instead of looking at this phenomenon through the lens of managers convincing the employees to return to the workplace and the employees not being interested, we should engage the situation in a way that all stakeholders examine, in co-opetition, the appropriate synchronization of the two spheres. For years, the goal was work–family balance, as in engagement in multiple roles with an approximately equal level of attention, time, involvement, or commitment (Greenhaus et al., 2003; Kirchmeyer, 2000). Employees felt that this goal was an empty statement, feeling that organizations try to pull them toward their work at the expense of their family. The Great Resignation signals to organizations that this goal of equal distribution is no longer necessarily true for all employees; each employee is interested in a different balance. Only when we understand that work and family stakeholders must work in co-opetition and find the right balance for each partner can we overcome the Great Resignation phenomenon and move toward a new future, a future of synchronization and not equilibrium (neither as a declared goal nor even as a sincere goal).

Nowadays, most families are dual-earner families and therefore, must manage the interfaces between two workplaces and the family, one interface related to the man's workplace and one related to the woman's workplace. Not only is there competition between the work and family domains in each interface, but the couple in the dual-earner family also must deal with the conflict created between the two workplaces. For example, when a child in the family is ill, a dilemma arises as to which of the parents should stay home and miss work. Successful management of this complex interface of two workplaces and one family in co-operation can minimize the conflict between the three systems (the man's work, the woman's work, and their family). Dual-earner family co-opetition appears on two levels: the co-opetition of each work and family interface and the co-opetition of the interface between the two work spheres and one family. This dual-earner work and family system (man's work, woman's work, and family) includes various stakeholders who manage the interface and therefore, should manage the co-opetition. In the next chapter, we detail the work and family co-opetition system stakeholders.

References

Allen, T. D., & Armstrong, J. (2006). Further examination of the link between work-family conflict and physical health: The role of health-related behaviors. *American Behavioral Scientist, 49*(9), 1204–1221.

Allen, T. D., Johnson, R. C., Kiburz, K. M., & Shockley, K. M. (2013). Work–family conflict and flexible work arrangements: Deconstructing flexibility. *Personnel Psychology, 66*(2), 345–376.

Arthur, M. B. (1994). The boundaryless career: A new perspective for organizational inquiry. *Journal of Organizational Behavior, 15*(4), 295–306.

Bailyn, L., Drago, R., & Kochan, T. A. (2001). *Integrating work and family life: A holistic approach.* Massachusetts Institute of Technology, Sloan School of Management.

Barnett, R. C., & Hyde, J. S. (2001). Women, men, work, and family: An expansionist theory. *American Psychologist, 56*(10), 781–796.

Barnett, R. C., Marshall, N. L., & Pleck, J. H. (1992). Men's multiple roles and their relationship to men's psychological distress. *Journal of Marriage and the Family, 54*(2), 358–367.

Bouziri, H., Smith, D. R., Descatha, A., Dab, W., & Jean, K. (2020). Working from home in the time of COVID-19: How to best preserve occupational health? *Occupational and Environmental Medicine, 77*(7), 509–510.

Brandenburger, A. M., & Nalebuff, B. J. (1996). *Co-opetition.* Harvard Business School Press.

Bruce, W., & Reed, C. (1994). Preparing supervisors for the future work force: The dual-income couple and the work-family dichotomy. *Public Administration Review, 54*(1), 36–43.

Carlson, D. S., Kacmar, K. M., & Williams, L. J. (2000). Construction and initial validation of a multidimensional measure of work–family conflict. *Journal of Vocational Behavior, 56*(2), 249–276.

Edwards, J. R., & Rothbard, N. P. (2000). Mechanisms linking work and family: Clarifying the relationship between work and family constructs. *Academy of Management Review, 25*(1), 178–199.

Ernst Kossek, E., & Ozeki, C. (1998). Work–family conflict, policies, and the job–life satisfaction relationship: A review and directions for organizational behavior–human resources research. *Journal of Applied Psychology, 83*(2), 139–149.

Fletcher, J., & Bailyn, L. (1996). Challenging the last boundary: Reconnecting work and family. In M. B. Arthur & D. M. Rousseau (Eds.), *The boundaryless career: A new employment principle for a new organizational era* (pp. 256–267). Oxford University Press.

Frone, M. R., Russell, M., & Cooper, M. L. (1992). Antecedents and outcomes of work-family conflict: Testing a model of the work-family interface. *Journal of Applied Psychology, 77*(1), 65–78.

Goode, W. J. (1960). A theory of role strain. *American Sociological Review, 25*, 483–496.

Greenhaus, J. H., Allen, T. D., & Spector, P. E. (2006). Health consequences of work–family conflict: The dark side of the work–family interface. In P. L. Perrewé & D. C. Ganster (Eds.), *Employee health, coping and methodologies* (pp. 61–98). Emerald Group.

Greenhaus, J. H., & Beutell, N. J. (1985). Sources of conflict between work and family roles. *Academy of Management Review, 10*(1), 76–88.

Greenhaus, J. H., Collins, K. M., & Shaw, J. D. (2003). The relation between work–family balance and quality of life. *Journal of Vocational Behavior, 63*(3), 510–531.

Greenhaus, J. H., & Powell, G. N. (2006). When work and family are allies: A theory of work-family enrichment. *Academy of Management Review, 31*, 72–92.

Grzywacz, J. G. (2000). Work-family spillover and health during midlife: is managing conflict everything? *American Journal of Health Promotion, 14*(4), 236–243.

Grzywacz, J. G., & Bass, B. L. (2003). Work, family, and mental health: Testing different models of work-family fit. *Journal of Marriage and Family, 65*(1), 248–261.

Halpern, D. F., & Murphy, S. E. (Eds.). (2013). *From work-family balance to work-family interaction: Changing the metaphor.* Routledge.

Jiskrova, G. K. (2022). Impact of COVID-19 pandemic on the workforce: From psychological distress to the Great Resignation. *Journal of Epidemiology & Community Health.* Advance online publication. https://doi.org/10.1136/jech-2022-218826

Kalliath, P. (2014). Is work–family enrichment an antidote to experiences of psychological strain among Australian social workers? An empirical study. *Australian Social Work, 67*(3), 332–347.

Kirchmeyer, C. (2000). Work-life initiatives: Greed or benevolence regarding workers' time? *Trends in Organizational Behavior, 7*, 79–94.

Kluwer, E. S., Heesink, J. A., & Van de Vliert, E. (1996). Marital conflict about the division of household labor and paid work. *Journal of Marriage and the Family, 58*(4), 958–969.

Kossek, E. E., Pichler, S., Bodner, T., & Hammer, L. B. (2011). Workplace social support and work–family conflict: A meta-analysis clarifying the influence of general and work–family-specific supervisor and organizational support. *Personnel Psychology, 64*(2), 289–313.

Marks, S. R. (1977). Multiple roles and role strain: Some notes on human energy, time and commitment. *American Sociological Review, 42*(6), 921–936.

Moen, P., Kaduk, A., Kossek, E. E., Hammer, L., Buxton, O. M., O'Donnell, Almeida, D., Fox, K., Tranby, E., Oakes, J. M., & Casper, L. (2015). Is work-family conflict a multilevel stressor linking job conditions to mental health? Evidence from the work, family and health network. In S. K. Ammons & E. L. Kelly (Eds.), *Work and family in the new economy* (pp. 177–217). Emerald Group.

Netemeyer, R. G., Boles, J. S., & McMurrian, R. (1996). Development and validation of work–family conflict and family–work conflict scales. *Journal of Applied Psychology, 81*(4), 400–410.

Parasuraman, S., & Greenhaus, J. H. (Eds.). (1999). *Integrating work and family: Challenges and choices for a changing world*. Greenwood.

Perry-Jenkins, M., Repetti, R. L., & Crouter, A. C. (2000). Work and family in the 1990s. *Journal of Marriage and Family, 62*(4), 981–998.

Pleck, J. H., Staines, G. L., & Lang, L. (1980). Conflicts between work and family life. *Monthly Labor Review, 103*, 29.

Powell, G. N., & Eddleston, K. A. (2013). Linking family-to-business enrichment and support to entrepreneurial success: Do female and male entrepreneurs experience different outcomes? *Journal of Business Venturing, 28*(2), 261–280.

Rantanen, J., Kinnunen, U., Mauno, S., & Tement, S. (2013). Patterns of conflict and enrichment in work-family balance: A three-dimensional typology. *Work & Stress, 27*(2), 141–163.

Ring, P. S., & Van de Ven, A. H. (1994). Developmental processes of cooperative interorganizational relationships. *Academy of Management Review, 19*(1), 90–118.

Sieber, S. D. (1974). Toward a theory of role accumulation. *American sociological review*, 567–578.

Tavares, A. I. (2017). Telework and health effects review. *International Journal of Healthcare, 3*(2), 30–36.

Xiao, Y., Becerik-Gerber, B., Lucas, G., & Roll, S. C. (2021). Impacts of working from home during COVID-19 pandemic on physical and mental well-being of office workstation users. *Journal of Occupational and Environmental Medicine, 63*(3), 181–190.

Chapter 2
Work–Family Stakeholders

Family resilience is part of work superiority, and work resilience allows
family completeness and togetherness generates well-being.
– Authors

A basic definition of the term "stakeholder" was presented by Varvasovsky and Brugha (2000), who defined stakeholders as "actors who have an interest in the issue under consideration, who are affected by the issue, or who – because of their position – have or could have an active or passive influence on the decision-making and implementation process" (p. 341). According to Parmar et al. (2010), stakeholders are individuals or groups who are influenced by or have an influence on the activities of the organization. A common definition was suggested by Clarkson (1995), who defined stakeholders as "persons or groups that have, or claim, ownership, rights, or interests in a corporation and its activities, past, present or future" (p. 98).

The term stakeholders can be differentiated into primary and secondary groups. A primary stakeholder group involves those whose continuing participation is essential to the organization's survival. It includes managers, employees, customers, investors, and suppliers on the one hand and public stakeholders, such as the government and communities that provide infrastructure, on the other. The secondary stakeholder group refers to those who influence or are influenced by a corporation but are not engaged in transactions and not essential for its survival. For instance, the media and a wide range of special interest groups are considered secondary stakeholders under this definition (Clarkson, 1995; Parmar et al., 2010).

Another categorization is based on boundary classification, describing stakeholders according to their position in the organization. Some are internal to the organization, such as executive managers, boards of directors, ethics committees, and company departments (financial, marketing, human resources, etc.); some are external, such as shareholders, suppliers, the local community, and the surrounding environment; and some are defined as interface stakeholders. Interface stakeholders are linked to both the internal and external environments. Interface stakeholders are distinct from internal or external stakeholders because they interact across boundaries and function both internally and externally (Clarkson, 1995; Dansky & Gamm, 2004; Harrison & St. John, 1996; Parmar et al., 2010). Scholars in the field of work and family have studied different stakeholders, such as governments, firms, community, unions, and family (Bailyn et al., 2001; Lewis & Cooper, 1999; Parasuraman & Greenhaus, 1999). In the present book, we highlight both the organizational environment and the stakeholders it has to consider when managing the work–family interface.

Regarding any organization-related phenomenon, any observer – whether manager, employee, human resources practitioner, or consultant – must consider it on at least

https://doi.org/10.1515/9783110759808-002

three levels: (a) individual; (b) team, group, or department; and (c) organization. Only when we assess an event, behavior, or performance at these three levels can we understand how things happen, how to respond, and with what methods to respond. Analyzing these levels will help us recognize the consequences and focus on the accurate and optimal reaction. By doing so, we view work and family stakeholders at all three levels as primary stakeholders.

Figure 2.1 shows the existing interface among the three levels: individual, team, and organization interacting with the individuals' families. The employee and his family are, seemingly, an independent unit but in reality, they are an inseparable part of the work-family spheres. Team leaders and members are also seemingly far away from employee's family; however, in reality, they are part of a strong interface that is not easy to separate. Finally, an organization contains teams and employees and consequently, is part of the inseparable context of employees and their families.

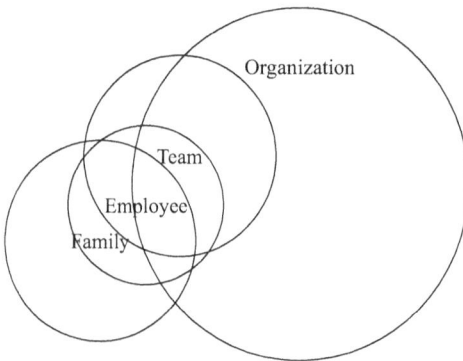

Figure 2.1: Three-level work–family interface.

Regarding dual-earner families, there is general agreement that today's workplaces need to include a broad range of activities taking into account family dynamics among employees. The interaction between work and family has gone through several recent changes. Social, technological, financial, and economic changes intensified by COVID-19 have led many companies to undertake unique strategies as a means of gaining and sustaining a competitive advantage. Consequently, companies are coping with demographic trends, social diversity, and social values and norms, which are reflected in the social structures of organizational systems (human resources management) and managerial practices toward employees and their families. The importance of employees to the organization, especially talented employees, has grown, and the need to consider their families has increased accordingly. Human resources management practices ranging from recruitment and selection through socialization, training, rewards, and welfare activities have been conducted. Yet these practices suggest a paternalistic point of view in the beginning, then place employees in the center, and only later account for employees' families and their needs. However, these practices failed to consider the daily interface, most of the time, of dual-earner families. Indeed, for the daily interface, the direct manager is of great significance, but even the direct manager is guided by organizational policies and practices.

Tzafrir and his colleagues (2013) mentioned that the organizational social environment involves any relationships between the organization and its members in the omnibus and discrete contexts. These relationships operate simultaneously at several levels: individual, team, and organization (Johns, 2006), including families. The organizational and employee social environments (Tzafrir et al., 2015) play a significant role in directing organizational, team, and individual effective behaviors and success. Tzafrir and his colleagues (2015) suggested that the "employment social arena is a microfoundation (Barney & Felin, 2013) representing individuals' characteristics, various forms of social interactions, and the process dynamics involved in different levels of organizational analysis" (p. 137). Thus, it is essential that these players develop awareness, policies, practices, and activities for coping with the challenges of work–family spheres. Following that, we suggest that at the organizational level, a fruitful interaction between work and family is an organizational value, views family as the basic unit instead of an individual employee, and represents a family-centered philosophy. At the team level, constraints resulting from one sphere, work or family, should be handled with balance among team members, symbolizing the notion of being a fundamental part of the team and allocation of friendly, thoughtful, and synchronized activities toward an employee's family (family friendly). At the individual level, work–family commitments must be in accordance with the uniqueness of each individual and family; therefore, a personalized synchronization in needed for each triangle. In sum, it is important for organizations to have clear policy, operate in a systematic method, and build team and managerial support. By doing so, these organization will recalculate their past policy (often organization-centered or employee-centered) toward adopting new social values (family-centered), thus adjusting organizational values to environmental changes. In the past, organizations have dealt with work–family conflict by moving toward work–family balance, and now they are required to look for work–family synchronization as a key tool for existence.

Organization and Work–Family Synchronization

A family-centered philosophy is a holistic norm that represents the significance of an employee's family in such a way that organizational activities recognize the existence of families simultaneously as potential organizational assets and challenges. We define family-centered philosophy as the compatibility of work and family values between the focal employees and their families and other organizational entities such as the human resources system, managers, coworkers, work team, and the entire organization. First, a family-centered philosophy must align individual and work values at the three different levels and activities. Second, a family-centered philosophy refers to a holistic understanding of the organization as part of society. Finally, a family-centered philosophy is mainly treated as synchronized and harmonized.

This upper-echelon philosophy leads organizations to consider both employee's behaviors in the family and the family's needs from the organization when it comes to establishing a human resources management policy addressing, among other things, the patterns of employee family assistance programs. In the past, priorities and practices toward the family were minor, if any existed. Later, organizations began to address issues of diversity as a result of demographic changes, challenges, and legislation. The issue of diversity has gained attention mainly regarding gender, disabilities, minorities, sexual orientation, and other disadvantaged groups. Despite their importance, families have received less organizational consideration. Today, it is clear to everyone that employees' families are of great importance to employees' attitudes, intentions, and behaviors. Accordingly, organizations invest great effort in coping with this relationship to achieve better productivity. Senior management and human resources systems are required, at the organizational level, to provide a substantive response to this acute challenge without giving up organizational objectives – for example, providing a clear statement about working hours, outlining various options regarding vacations, building teams from an understanding of diversity, etc. The crucial point is the organizational ability to concurrently clarify the organizational vision, mission, and objectives and understand the family's unique dynamics for various generations, diverse stages of life, and different families. In doing so, a human resources system might make office adjustments or allow employees to work from home to ensure synchronization with family's responsibilities. How to assess whether employees manage to meet their personal and organizational goals while preserving well-being will require modification in the employee assessment system. As a result, human resources departments are required to evaluate employees based on results in parallel with teamwork qualities and contributions, meeting deadlines, controlling family challenges, and accessing organizational support.

Organizations that want to have a family-friendly standard must treat time flexibly in terms of working hours and meetings based on their employees' discretion, all within the organizational and departmental contexts. This does not mean organizational anarchy; the opposite is true. What is required is a trust-based culture that allows autonomy and discretion out of mutual agreement on clear and defined boundaries of practices, actions, and behaviors. Hence, in today's world, one clear organizational challenge is to build a system of trust between employees and the organization – one that allows employees to feel comfortable raising a problem, making an offer, making risky decisions, and contacting senior managers when needed and at the same time, allows the organization to communicate to employees to increase their effort and strive harder when needed. Such a system that considers the family will lead to diffuse efforts from one entity to another and thus, will cause the employee's family to be an additional asset for the organization in complex and difficult times such as the COVID-19 pandemic.

Team and Work–Family Synchronization

A family-friendly team symbolizes the notion of an employee's family as a fundamental part of the work team. A family-friendly team is defined as a group whose members, including the employee's family, have complementary practices and are committed to common goals for both the team and family for which they hold themselves mutually responsible. Organizations are adopting or improving such a structure to produce concrete and exceptional performance. The team should assist and support employees in coping with family needs and requirements, and employee should give maximum effort toward achieving the team's goals.

A family-friendly team recognizes the employee's family as an integral part of it and takes steps to act and conduct practices for families as if they were team members. A family-friendly team culture of trust will lead both the team leader and members to recognize the process of ongoing interaction between their activities in the team and their activities in the family, and so on. A positive team circulation process depends on the openness of all members in both spheres, work and family. Processes, actions, and practices are diffused between team and family due to various contexts and objectives. Metaphorically, think of this circulation process as occurring through a net. A fishnet, for example, separates fish from the sea. The permeability of such net defines the level of diffusion between team members and their families, and it may be affected by the team's practices and norms. The size of the holes affects the possible diffusion of activities from one sphere to another. For instance, if an employee is allowed to work from home but cannot take with him a computer from work, then work will have a lesser (there are always thoughts about work) or no effect when staying at home. If trust exists in cooperation in the team and between the team and family members, it allows all stakeholders to pay attention to the reciprocal demands of the work–family spheres. Therefore, such a psychological contract will deal with work–family mixture and the relationship intensity between the manager and the employee's spouse, for instance. Managers should look for a sense that the family is part of the organization and team, consider family in management decisions, and simultaneously allow flexibility among employees to decide how to manage the interface between work and family.

The ability of the whole team to work together and accept the fact that there are other factors, including family, that affect its activities will help the team achieve its goals and perform better than the sum of its parts. Part of this high performance is due to the ability to concentrate while working because of awareness that the family is fine and when needed, employees can be with their family and the team leader and members will support them. Such awareness helps team members manage their time, navigate their effort, and cope with demanding goals while reducing the friction between members both on the individual and group levels. A family-friendly team values family similar to other social values that are perceived as universal (e.g., equality, justice), thus helping build respect and shared pride among team members and between families and the team. That is, trust enables a respectful relationship among team members, and this respectful relationship increases trust among members. The result is a positive cycle of trust that leads to passing significant and accurate information at the right time, more cooperative friendships and partnerships, and mutual support resulting in improved performance, innovation, creativity, and efficiency. These harmonized work–family spheres create a pleasant and enjoyable work environment and well-being, as opposed to a toxic environment, helping the team cope in a complex and dynamic organizational environment that requires them to do more with fewer resources.

Individuals and Work–Family Synchronization

At the organizational level, we demonstrated how an organizational philosophy should emphasize the importance of the employee and their family to the organizational vision. At the team level, we emphasized the need to act in a way that sees the family as an integral part of the team. That is, employees and their families are at the center as part of a holistic rationale. Such a rationale is important and requires taking one more managerial step in light of the tremendous diversity that exists among individuals in the labor market. At the individual level, managers must pay attention to each employee as unique, given the great diversity of individuals and different family preferences. One team member is not identical to another, and one family is not the equivalent as another. Therefore, it is necessary to tailor a specific personalized suit (e.g. work policies, procedures, practices, benefits, salary, responsibilities) for each team member in accordance with their individual characteristics, marital status, relevant job context, and time.

The relationship between an employee (team member), team, manager (team leader), and organization is not a symmetrical relationship, suggesting the need to create balance to deal with the asymmetry. Generating a balanced relationship is motivating in that at its core is the assumption that conflict can be overcome. In a sense, the desire to create a balance between the two spheres of family and work may lead to the illusion that the inherent conflict between the two can be eliminated. Objectively, the reality is that each day of the week has 24 hours that an individual can divide between family, work, and other activities. In this sense, an hour devoted to work, in many cases, cannot be devoted to family; thus, a built-in conflict exists, at least in terms of time. Thus, balance is good but not enough; we need to do more to manage the situation. Synchronization between all entities involved in the situation is essential. It is necessary to create a perception of stability that allows the spouse to perceive and maintain work needs in parallel with family needs, using a calculation-based system in a psychological contract agreed upon by the couple. In the workplace, the ability to rely on team members and leaders and gain their support when needed in dynamic situations requiring agility will increase an employee's sense of resilience. In turn, this resilience will allow employees to deal positively with power asymmetries, increase self-efficacy, and allow positive responses to family needs. This double action creates a positive feeling in the employee that leads to higher performance in complex and uncertainty situations. Hence, an employee's ability to better synchronize between work and family allows them to better cope with many pressures exerted on them on both levels.

To manage the individual level, we have to recognize the three stakeholders who handle the daily work–family interface – the manager, the employee, and the employee's spouse – and explore their tripartite relationship. From the organizational point of view, the manager can be perceived as an internal stakeholder, the employee's spouse as an external stakeholder, and the employee as an interface stakeholder who mediates and negotiates between work (internal) and family (external). As noted, we perceive these three as primary stakeholders.

This perception of the employee's spouse as part of the employee–manager relationship is novel and contradicts the perception that the concept of career is an individual concept, rooted in ideas of individual choice, fit, and tradeoffs (Fletcher & Bailyn, 1996). We view career as a systemic concept, rooted in an appreciation of the interdependent nature of organizational and individual concerns and of work and family. Through this systematic lens, the employee's career is interdependent on both the manager and spouse and therefore, three important players influence the employee's career path: manager, employee, and employee's spouse. As Friedlander (1994) noted, the irony is that although there is a growing awareness that companies must be viewed as entities operating in larger societal and global systems when it comes to work and family, the view of individuals remains narrowly focused and tightly bounded in the public sphere, with little recognition of the family, community, and societal systems in which all individuals operate. This is true today as it was in 1994.

This is in line with Voydanoff (2014), who demonstrated that demands and resources associated with one domain (work or family) have important effects on the role performance and quality of life in the other, either directly or through mediating mechanisms. We argue that one main mediator is the employee's spouse and therefore, we view the spouse as a primary stakeholder. The spouses' role as a primary stakeholder is rooted in (a) their direct influence on the employee, (b) the information they have regarding the suitable arrangement of work and family, (c) the extent to which they feel valued in their work and family relationships and not as an outsider who has to "pay the price," and (d) their role in the couple's strategies regarding work and family relationships that should be considered when developing work and family arrangements.

Spouse Influence

Family systems theory (Minuchin, 1974) proposes that an individual's actions are affected by the actions of other primary actors in the family (e.g., spouse and children). This means that the employee's spouse is an important key player in the work–family interface. Fellows et al. (2016) examined the association between work–family conflict and couple relationship quality, conducting a meta-analytic review of 49 samples from 33 papers published between 1986 and 2014. The results indicated a significant negative relationship between work–family conflict and couple relationship quality. In addition, many studies on couples who relocated internationally examined the spouse's influence on the willingness and adjustment of the employee (Brett, 1982; Konopaske et al., 2005). Therefore, the spouse's influence is of utmost relevance in the entire work–family interface, and studies must consider them as stakeholders in the work and family co-opetition system.

Spouse Information

Organizations that are sufficiently wise integrate stakeholders into their decision-making strategy (Parmar et al., 2010). One clear added value of stakeholders is that they have important and necessary information that we have to take into account. They present different perspectives, experiences, and expertise when involved in the process of making strategic decisions. If the information is well captured by the decision makers, it will lead to a better organizational performance (Mortelmans et al., 2006). Accordingly, the employee's spouse has information that is necessary for an effective co-opetition system. For example, the manager and employee may decide to postpone a long business trip from a holiday period to the following month, as a family gesture, not considering that for the spouse, a business trip on school days is a considerably heavier burden because it means the spouse has to handle the children's daily activities alone.

Spouse Esteem

Stakeholders who feel that managers and senior directors have considered their opinions and interests will be more committed to the organization and develop a feeling of ownership, which in turn, will motivate them and improve both their performance and the organization's performance (Parmar et al., 2010). In line with this, it is desirable that all stakeholders feel that the work and family relationship is conducted as a co-opetition relationship and not a war. Moreover, they should feel like part of a relationship that aims to find a way to minimize conflict and maximize enrichment. For this purpose, spouses need to feel that they have an important role in the relationship, that their interests are the relationship's interests, and that without them, the arrangement would be incomplete.

Couple Strategies

Working couples use different strategies to manage work and life pressures (Becker & Moen, 1999; Greenhaus & Powell, 2017; Moen, 2003). It is becoming increasingly evident that work and family strategies are typically family-level actions and fluid, emergent processes (Marks & MacDermid, 1996; Moen & Wethington, 1992; Moen & Yu, 2000). In the case of dual-earner families, the strategy is even more complicated. It must address not only two competing roles (work and family), but three-way juggling: his work, her work (dealing with two managers), and their family goals and responsibilities. The focus should be on couple-level lines of adaptation and how they shift or remain constant over the life course.

Couples should decide on their temporal and emotional investment in work. Some couples who seek to maximize both of their careers can be expected to work long hours, hold high status (professional or managerial) jobs, and give high priority to each of their jobs. Studies have described couple strategies of reducing the family demand side of the work–family equation by postponing childbearing and reducing family size (Clarkberg, 1999; Moen, 2003). The rising number of nannies and au pairs points to another strategy for those who can afford it: in essence, hiring a "wife" (Hochschild, 1999). Other couples put both careers on the back burner, giving primacy to the other aspects of their lives. This can be either a deliberate choice or because they lack the human capital or opportunity to do otherwise (Greenhaus & Powell, 2017; Moen, 2003). Another strategy is the compensatory strategy, where one spouse focuses on paid work while the other spouse invests more in the domestic aspects of their lives. The evidence suggests that the model of compensatory action is typical of most dual-earner couples (Becker & Moen, 1999; Blossfeld & Hakim, 1997).

All these strategies are couple, not individual employee, strategies. Therefore, we argue that organizations in the macro aspect and managers in the micro aspect must view the spouse as an important interface stakeholder, a primary stakeholder, and a stakeholder who influences the work–family couple strategy, which of course, influences the employee's work. This book reveals different strategies that couples adopt and the dynamics between their strategy and the direct employee–manager relationship.

Having elaborated on four reasons that bolster the argument that the spouse is a primary stakeholder, we conclude that three stakeholders manage the daily work–family interface: (a) manager, (b) employee, and (c) employee's spouse, each guided by laws, social rules, and organizational policies and practices. These three are best represented in a triangle relationship, as depicted in Figure 2.2. In a dual-earner family, there are four stakeholders who are distinguished by their different, and sometimes conflicting, interests: (a) woman, (b) man, (c) woman's manager, and (d) man's manager. The four are best represented as two adjacent triangles, the work–family triangle of the woman and the work–family triangle of the man. They create a work–family triangle system as depicted in Figure 2.3 that has to manage the work–family interface.

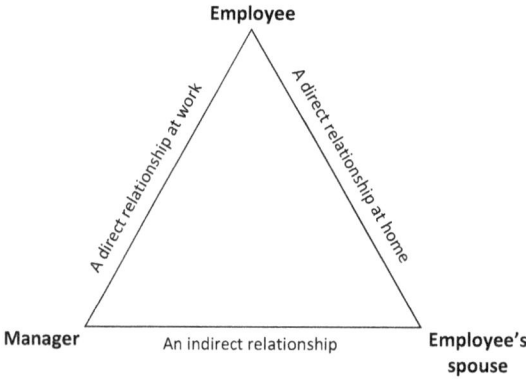

Figure 2.2: Work–family triangle stakeholders.

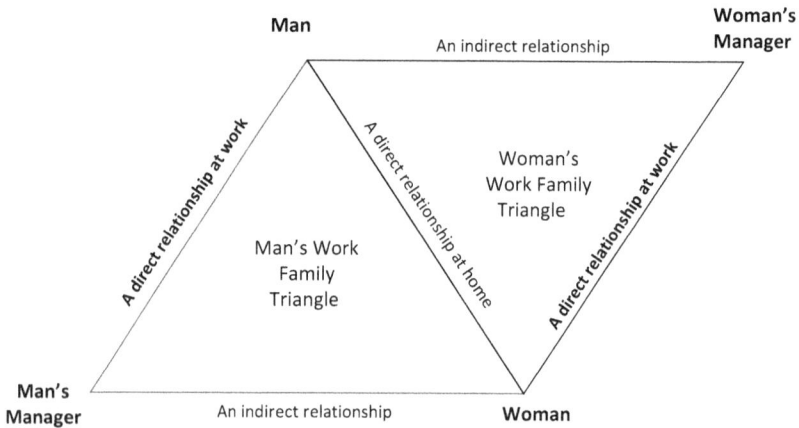

Figure 2.3: Dual-earner work–family triangle system stakeholders.

This work–family triangle system goal is to generate a productive and healthy environment in all spheres and for all stakeholders. This goal is attained through the different triangle dyads. The next chapter elaborates on these dyads and the way they interrelate

New Concepts in the Chapter
- *Family-centered philosophy* – The compatibility of work and family values between the focal employees and their families and other organizational entities such as the human resources system, managers, coworkers, work team, and organization.
- *Family-friendly team* – A group whose members, including the employee's family, have complementary practices and are committed to common goals for both the team and family for which they hold themselves mutually responsible.

References

Bailyn, L., Drago, R., & Kochan, T. A. (2001). Integrating work and family life. *A Holistic Approach, A Report of the Sloan Work-Family Policy Network: MIT, Sloan School of Management*.

Barney, J. A. Y., & Felin, T. (2013). What are microfoundations? *Academy of Management Perspectives*, *27*(2), 138–155.

Becker, P. E., & Moen, P. (1999). Scaling back: Dual-earner couples' work-family strategies. *Journal of Marriage and the Family*, 995–1007

Blossfeld, H. P., & Hakim, C. (1997). *Between equalization and marginalization: women working part-time in Europe*. Oxford University Press.

Brett, J. M. (1982). Job transfer and well-being. *Journal of Applied Psychology*, *67*(4), 450.

Clarkberg, M. (1999). The price of partnering: The role of economic well-being in young adults' first union experiences. *Social Forces*, *77*(3), 945–968.

Clarkson, M. E. (1995). A stakeholder framework for analyzing and evaluating corporate social performance. *Academy of management review*, *20*(1), 92–117.

Dansky, K. H., & Gamm, L. S. (2004). Accountability framework for managing stakeholders of health programs. *Journal of health organization and management*, *18*(4), 290–304.

Fellows, K. J., Chiu, H. Y., Hill, E. J., & Hawkins, A. J. (2016). Work–family conflict and couple relationship quality: A meta-analytic study. *Journal of Family and Economic Issues*, *37*(4), 509–518.

Fletcher, J., & Bailyn, L. (1996). Challenging the last boundary: Reconnecting work and family. *The boundaryless career: A new employment principle for a new organizational era*, 256–267.

Friedlander, F. (1994). Toward whole systems and whole people. *Organization*, *1*(1), 59–64.

Greenhaus, J. H., & Powell, G. N. (2017) *Making Work and Family Work: From hard choices to smart choices*. Routledge.

Harrison, J. S., & St. John, C. H. (1996). Managing and partnering with external stakeholders. *Academy of Management Perspectives*, *10*(2), 46–60.

Hochschild, A. (1999). The Nanny Chain. American Prospect 11:32–36. Huber.

Johns, G. (2006). The essential impact of context on organizational behavior. *Academy of management review*, *31*(2), 386–408.

Konopaske, R., Robie, C., & Ivancevich, J. M. (2005). A preliminary model of spouse influence on managerial global assignment willingness. *The International Journal of Human Resource Management*, *16*(3), 405–426.

Lewis, S., & Cooper, C. L. (1999). The work-family research agenda in changing contexts. Journal of Occupational Health Psychology. 4. 382–392.

Marks, S. R., & MacDermid, S. M. (1996). Multiple roles and the self: A theory of role balance. *Journal of Marriage and the Family*, 417–432.

Minuchin, S. (1974) Families and Family Therapy. Cambridge, MA: Harvard Univ.

Moen, P. (2003). *It's about time: Couples and careers*. Cornell University Press.

Moen, P., & Wethington, E. (1992). The concept of family adaptive strategies. Annual review of sociology, 233–251.

Moen, P., & Yu, Y. (2000). Effective work/life strategies: Working couples, work conditions, gender, and life quality. *Social problems*, *47*(3), 291–326.

Mortelmans, K., Donceel, P., & Lahaye, D. (2006). Disability management through positive intervention in stakeholders' information asymmetry. A pilot study. *Occupational Medicine*, *56*(2), 129–136.

Parasuraman, S., & Greenhaus, J. H. (Eds.). (1999). *Integrating work and family: Challenges and choices for a changing world*. Greenwood Publishing Group.

Parmar, B. L., Freeman, R. E., Harrison, J. S., Wicks, A. C., Purnell, L., & De Colle, S. (2010). Stakeholder theory: The state of the art. *The academy of management annals*, *4*(1), 403–445.

Tzafrir, S., Enosh, G., Parry, E., & Stone, D. (2013). CODIFYing social issues in organizations: Scope and perspectives. *Global Business Perspectives*, *1*(1), 39–47.

Tzafrir, S. S., Gur, A. B. A., & Blumen, O. (2015). Employee social environment (ESE) as a tool to decrease intention to leave. *Scandinavian Journal of Management*, *31*(1), 136–146.

Varvasovszky, Z., & Brugha, R. (2000). A stakeholder analysis. *Health policy and planning*, *15*(3), 338–345.

Voydanoff, P. (2014). *Work, family, and community: Exploring interconnections*. Psychology Press.

Chapter 3
Work–Family Triangle's Dyads

> Your imagination is your preview of life's coming attractions.
> – Albert Einstein

The work–family interface can and should be managed as a triangles system. When organizations and families understand the dynamic of the triangles and address the work–family interface as a triangles system, they can imagine how this conflict interface can be managed through co-opetition and not competition. In the previous chapter, we elaborated on the stakeholders who manage the daily interface events. Now it is time to examine the dyads that manage the daily work–family interface: (1) manager–employee dyad, (2) couple dyad, and (3) manager–employee's spouse dyad. The current chapter examines the dynamics of these three dyads and how stakeholders can act together as a team, and not everyone on their own, to manage conflict. It is not a cruel reality that we have to survive. It is a complex reality that we can and should manage for the benefit of all players.

The Direct Relationship at Work: The Manager–Employee Dyad

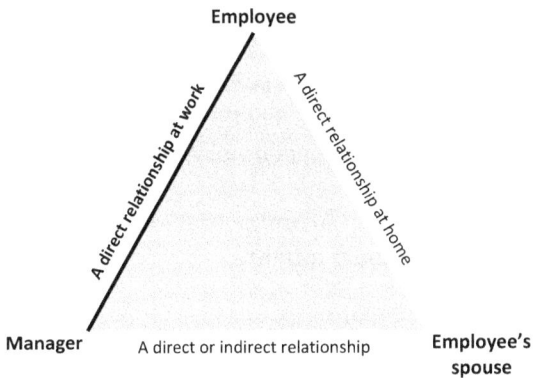

Figure 3.1: The direct relationship at work – the manager–employee dyad.

Figure 3.1 illustrates the direct relationship at work, the manager–employee dyad. This dyad is managed through both a written contract and a psychological contract. Rousseau (1989) defined a psychological contract as an "individual's belief regarding the terms and conditions of a reciprocal exchange agreement between that focal person and another party" (p. 123). Research on psychological contracts has revealed that although each party believes that both parties have accepted the same contract terms,

https://doi.org/10.1515/9783110759808-003

this does not necessarily mean that both parties share a common understanding of all the contract terms. Each party believes that the partner shares their interpretation of the contract (Baruch & Rousseau, 2019). Thus, psychological contracts are subjective, residing in the "eyes of the beholder" (Robinson & Rousseau, 1994, p. 246).

Our experience shows that this subjectivity is a key issue when managing the manager–employee dyad. In separate interviews, we found that in cases where the manager and employee had different perceptions regarding work and family needs and abilities, it led to different perceptions regarding the psychological contract between them and as a result, to greater tension. An example is the case of Liam and William.

> Liam, William's manager, refused his repeated requests to leave early, thinking William was exaggerating about how much his family needs him. Liam told us that William's wife can handle the family needs and let William work with no interference, whereas William knew his wife has a demanding job, too, and thought the family responsibilities have to be divided between both parents. Liam and William never talked about this openly with each other, but they both felt that there was a lot of tension regarding William's request to attend to home needs.

Researchers studying the psychological contract examined the implication of violating the contract. They found that when a contract is violated, it generates distrust, dissatisfaction, and possibly the dissolution of the relationship itself (Rousseau, 1989; Turnley & Feldman, 2000).

When the work–family psychological contract is understood differently, the perception that one actor (manager or employee) is violating the contract is unavoidable. In these cases, the actor that violated the contract did not understand the commotion. He didn't perceive his behavior as violating the contract. A familiar example is when a manager calls the employee at 11 p.m., thinking it is part of the 24/7 psychological contract, whereas the employee perceives it as a fundamental violation of the psychological contract that respects family time.

The manager–employee work–family psychological contract has to deal with two segments: **work–family hierarchy** and **work–family mixture**.

Work–Family Hierarchy

The **work–family hierarchy** segment deals with the challenging questions of which sphere makes the rules and which sphere needs to adjust. Which sphere has to help the other to ensure responsibilities and job demands are met? Does the family have to compromise and fit itself to work demands and enable the employee to do the job? Does the work have to compromise and adjust to the family needs to make it possible for the employee to manage the family role? The phenomenon can be drawn on a continuum from "work compromises and adjusts to family" to "family compromises and adjusts to work," as depicted in Figure 3.2.

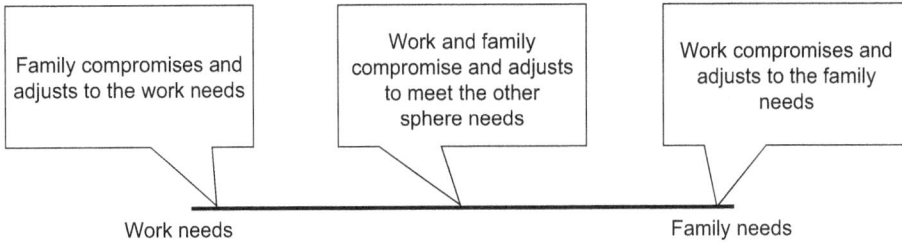

| Family compromises and adjusts to the work needs | Work and family compromise and adjusts to meet the other sphere needs | Work compromises and adjusts to the family needs |

Work needs   Family needs

Figure 3.2: Continuum of work–family hierarchy.

Some of the work and family adjustments are long-term decisions, such as place of residence. Those decisions are part of the couple's work–family psychological contract. The work–family hierarchy psychological contract of the manager–employee dyad is more about adjustments in daily situations, wherein work and family needs are in day-to-day conflict. For example, a couple intended to go out with friends in the evening, but there is a problem at work and the manager asked the employee to stay and handle the situation. If work adjusts to the family, the employee will apologize and say to his manager that he has a family obligation and cannot stay. If the family has to adjust to work, then the employee will call the spouse and apologize about canceling their plans. As we can see, the manager–employee work–family hierarchy psychological contract is tied together with the couple work–family hierarchy psychological contract. We expand on this understanding later in the chapter.

Sometimes the feeling is that the sphere that is higher in the hierarchy abuses the contract. In triangles where the work is above the family, a frequent feeling is that the manager defined every late meeting or business trip abroad as urgent or even an emergency. In triangle systems where the family is above the work in the hierarchy, the manager frequently feels that the employee is abusing the manager's consideration of the family and that every small family need means the employee leaves the workplace. These violations are part of the subjectivity of the contract.

It is important to understand that the work–family hierarchy does not address the question of which is more important, work or family. Managers, employees, and spouses typically state that the family is more important than work, and when there is a family crisis, such as hospitalization or a significant event involving a family member, the employee should be with the family and the workplace must allow it.

Work–Family Mixture

The **work–family mixture** segment deals with the extent to and intensity with which the two spheres interrelate. The spheres interrelate in three main areas:
(1) Handling family or work matters when at work or home: The extent to and intensity with which the employee handles family matters when at work, and vice versa.

(2) Talking about family or work with the manager or spouse: The extent to and intensity with which the employee talks about family with the manager and about work with the spouse.
(3) Attention placed on family or work matters while at work or home: The extent to and intensity with which the employee is occupied with family matters when at work and not fully focused on work, and vice versa.

When we analyze the extent and the intensity of these areas, we find that the work–family mixture is on a continuum from work–family separation through work–family interaction to work–family integration, as depicted in Figure 3.3.

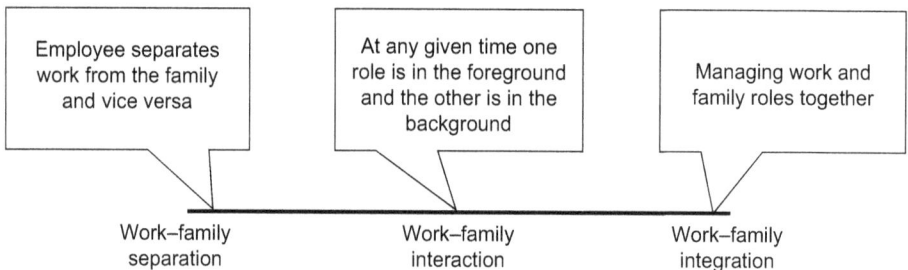

Figure 3.3: Continuum of work–family mixture .

Work–family separation means that the employee separates work from the family and vice versa. When the employee is at work, the employee is only at work and is not occupied with family matters, and vice versa. This includes not talking about family when at work and not talking about work when with family. The employee perceives the two spheres as two separate spheres and that one should not interfere with the other.

On the other end of the continuum, **work–family integration** is the state of mind that the best way to manage their two roles is to fill them together, as one of the employees stated:

> I am the mother of all my children at the same time. I love them and take care of them together. The exception is when I am with only one of them and think, talk, and do stuff only with him. Most of the time, I am with all of them together. It is the same with work and family. I handle family and work together. I work from home and answer work calls while I prepare lunch for my kids. I write emails when I breast-feed my little baby. Work and family today are blended, and many people struggle with it. I think we should embrace it. This is the new era.

Finally, **work–family interaction** exists between these two ends of the continuum; that is, there is interaction between the spheres, but they are not entirely blended. They are two spheres, and at any given time, one role is in the foreground and the other is in the background depending on the context. When the employee is at work, the main task is to be involved in work matters. Sometimes, when needed, the employee will take care of a family matter. The same applies when at home with family. The main role is the family, but sometimes the employee answers work calls and handles work matters.

The manager and the employee can perceive the desired work–family mixture differently. Ideally, when they are synchronized, there is no tension. When they are not synchronized, we witness difficulties. In one high-tech company we worked with, a manager–employee dyad demonstrated such a case.

> Jaxon, the employee, believed that there should be complete separation between work and family. He did not bring his wife to company events and did not talk about her at work. His manager saw this as a loyalty issue, thinking the work–family mixture should involve interaction and not separation. He did not understand how work was not a significant part of Jaxon's family life.

As in the work–family hierarchy segments, there is no correct approach that suits all managers and employees. The challenge in the work–family mixture is to synchronize between the manager and employee, understanding their different needs and abilities. That means that each manager has to identify the appropriate work–family mixture for each employee being managed. Who is available and willing to receive a call in the evening and who is not? Who will answer emails on the weekend and who will not? Which employee would like the company event to include families and who would prefer to avoid such events? Who wants to talk about family matters? Who would see it as invasive and maybe rude? Who would think that not showing interest means the manager does not care?

It is interesting to identify asymmetric cases in which employees separate work from family when they are at home but mix the spheres when they are at work. That means the work–family mixture is more complicated and context specific. The work–family mixture at work differs from the work–family mixture at home. They are not necessarily equal. In these cases, some managers feel deceived. This is another reason why the work–family mixture psychological contract has to be synchronized.

The manager–employee work–family psychological contract also is affected by changes in job security. A secure income is one of the most basic family needs. The fundamental shift away from long-term careers in one or two organizations, creates a mutual job insecurity in various industries that affects the manager–employee dyad. Both the manager and the employee have to make sure that the other is satisfied, otherwise either one can cancel the written contract – the manager can dismiss the employee or the employee can quit.

In cases where managers are sensitive to job security, they talk about complying with employees' work–family hierarchy and mixture even when they don't agree with it. The same is true for employees, agreeing to work during family time while adjusting the family needs to work demands because they were afraid it will affect their job security.

When the manager is unaware of an unsynchronized work–family psychological contract, it is difficult to meet the employees' needs, like in the example of Luke and Dylan.

Luke, the manager, thought that Dylan, his employee, would be happy that he took him off a big project so he could be available to his newborn child. Dylan was mad that Luke made the decision for him regarding the work–family hierarchy. Dylan preferred to continue the project at the expense of the family.

Understanding these challenges requires all actors to synchronize their work–family psychological contract. After synchronizing it, the manager and employee should translate it to work arrangements, flexibility of work hours, work-from-home options, and other adjustments to work demands or family needs. Chapter 6, WFS Triaxial Contract, describes how the players should build their own implementation of the work–family psychological contract.

The Couple (Employee–Spouse) Dyad

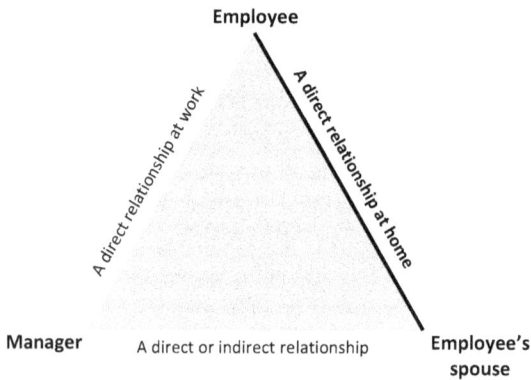

Figure 3.4: The direct relationship at home – the employee–spouse dyad.

Figure 3.4 illustrates the direct relationship at home – the employee–spouse dyad. Work and family studies have examined the employee–spouse relationship (Han & Moen, 1999; Huffman et al., 2014; Moen & Wethington, 1992; Pittman & Blanchard, 1996). Working couples use different strategies to manage work and life pressures (Becker & Moen, 1999; Greenhaus & Powell, 2017; Moen, 2003). It is becoming increasingly evident that work and family strategies are typically family-level actions and are fluid, emergent processes (Marks & MacDermid, 1996; Moen & Wethington, 1992; Moen & Yu, 2000).

In the case of dual-earner families, the strategy is even more complicated. It must address not only two competing roles (work and family), but a three-way juggling act: his work, her work, and their family goals and responsibilities. The focus should be on couple-level lines of adaptation and how they shift or, conversely, remain constant over the life course (Han & Moen, 1999). The couple work–family psychological contract has to deal with work–family mixture and work–family hierarchy, too. We found tension in cases wherein the couple was unsynchronized regarding these segments.

Work–Family Mixture

An example of an unsynchronized couple work–family psychological contract is that of Aiden and Leah.

> Leah thought there should be a separation between work and family (work–family mixture): "When you are at home with the family you should not handle work issues." Aiden, the employee, thought and acted otherwise. The couple frequently argued about this disparity whenever he answered calls and emails during dinner or family playtime.

The couple has to synchronize the work–family mixture, to consider that each triangle (the woman's work–family triangle and the man's work–family triangle) can have a different work–family mixture, like in the following example.

> The man was frustrated that whereas he talks a lot about his work with his wife, she does not share and consult with him regarding her work. He perceived that both work–family mixtures (his work and her work) should be characterized by work–family interaction, with significant sharing at home. She understood he needed to share and accepted that, but she didn't need to share.

Work–Family Hierarchy

Exploring the couple work–family psychological contract regarding the work–family-hierarchy, things are more complicated because they have to consider both workplaces.

Each triangle in the system (man's work–family triangle and woman's work–family triangle) has its work–family hierarchy and they both influence each other, creating a work–family triangles system hierarchy – a hierarchy of the man's work needs, the woman's work needs, and the family's needs. Part of the couple work–family psychological contract is to synchronize the triangles system work–family hierarchy.

An example of a synchronized triangles system work–family hierarchy is that of Anthony and Eva.

> Anthony is a doctor. Eva agreed to the work–family triangles system hierarchy contract that his work needs come before family needs and her work needs. When Anthony was with the children and was required at the hospital, Eva would return home from work or the activity in which she was engaged. In one case, Eva was at the beginning of an important meeting when Anthony called. He was required for a complicated surgery. She apologized to the client and returned home.

In cases involving working for the military, many couples are synchronized that the family has to adjust to the man's work (military) needs, placing the officer's work–family hierarchy on the "work needs" end of the continuum (see Figure 4.2), meaning that both the family and the woman's work (we found few cases where the man's work compromised for the woman's military work needs) compromise for and adjust to the military needs. Sometimes, this means moving from place to place every few years, and the spouse accepted this contract.

In such work–family triangles systems, it is clear that the man's work is higher in the hierarchy and sets the rules, the family adjusts to them, and the woman's work adjusts to them as a continuation of the chain. This situation is illustrated in Figure 3.5 and demonstrated in the following example.

Roman is a senior commander in the army. Eli, the woman's manager, told her frequently that he feels that he, too, serves the army, allowing her flexibility at work because of her husband's duty.

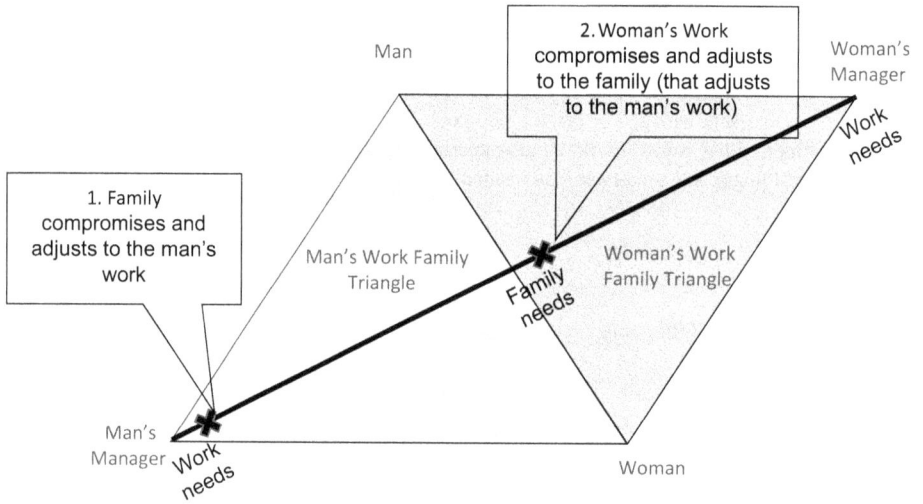

Figure 3.5: Family adjusts to the man's work and woman's work adjusts to family.

There are work–family triangles systems in which the family has to adjust to both work need – the man's and woman's work needs – as illustrated in Figure 3.6.

This is the case of the triangles system of Oliver and Emma, both officers in the army.

Oliver and Emma have a work–family hierarchy located on the work needs ends of the continuum. The family adjusts to both work needs. The main family need that was not fulfilled and had to adjust was the need of the children for a parent as a caregiver. Oliver and Emma know the price their family has to pay for their choices.

The couple work–family hierarchy affects the managers and therefore, has to synchronized with the manager–employee work–family hierarchy. In interviews, the managers of the women in "Man's World" triangles systems said that they (woman's manager) felt that the burden of adjusting to family is left on their shoulders because the man's work does not adjust – for example, when a child is sick or on vacation from school.

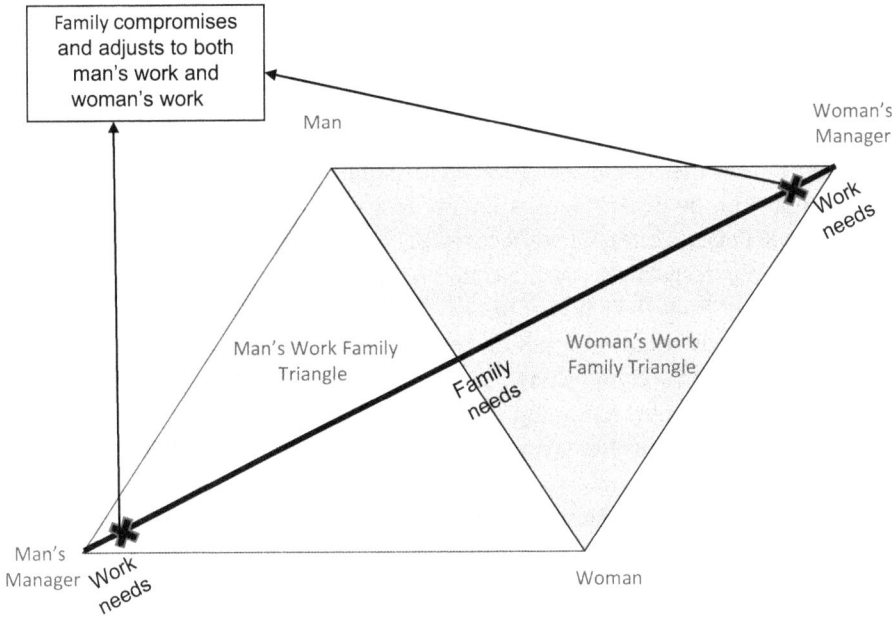

Figure 3.6: Family adjusts to both man's work and woman's work.

Situations wherein the manager feels the family needs to sacrifice and adjust its attention, time, and effort to work needs while one or both parents feel otherwise has the potential to lead to many conflicts (at both home and work). Many high-tech employees' spouses told us that this was a frequent cause of fights at home; for example, when the manager requested that the employee travel abroad when the family had plans or the employee had recently returned from a business trip.

Moreover, in some cases, because of work needs rather than family needs, the spouse's work had to adjust. For example, if the man, who usually takes the children to school in the mornings, has an early meeting or is on a business trip, then the woman has to take the children and might arrive late to work. The family needs, to which the man's work had adjusted, are now the needs to which the woman's work has to adjust because of the man's work needs. Again, we see the extent to which the two triangles interrelate. The dyads' work–family psychological contracts are tied together and have to be synchronized, too.

As noted in the manager–employee work–family hierarchy psychological contract, sometimes the feeling is that the higher sphere abuses the contract. The manager's perception of abuse sometimes involves the couple work–family hierarchy, as in this example:

Sarah was a doctorate student and Aaron was the supervisor. Aaron felt that the student's spouse denied the student's doctorate (work) needs for every family need and did not attempt to find a way whereby the doctorate needs would come first.

Work–Family Role

In addition to work–family hierarchy and work–family mixture, the couple work–family psychological contract has a third segment: work–family role. **Work–family role** refers to how the couple decides to divide family and work roles. Each member of the couple can be career focused, family focused, or career-and-family focused (Greenhaus & Powell, 2017). Career-focused people and family-focused people place work and family, respectively, at the center of their lives and derive their strongest sense of identity from their higher-priority role. Career-and-family-focused people place approximately equal emphasis on both roles and derive their sense of self from their experiences and accomplishments in both domains (Greenhaus & Powell, 2017).

As in the work–family hierarchy, the couple work–family psychological contract regarding work–family role has to consider both workplaces. Figure 3.7 maps the work–family roles of the work–family triangles systems on a coordinate system, wherein the X-axis is the man's work and family roles and the Y-axis is the woman's work and family roles. There are six types of triangles system work–family roles: (1) career-focused triangles system, in which both parents are career focused; (2) family-focused triangles system, in which both parents are family focused; (3) career-and-family-focused triangles system, in which both parents are career-and-family focused; (4) complementary triangles system, in which the man is career focused and the woman is family focused; (5) complementary triangles system, in which the woman is career focused and the man is family focused; and (6) reciprocal complementary triangles system,

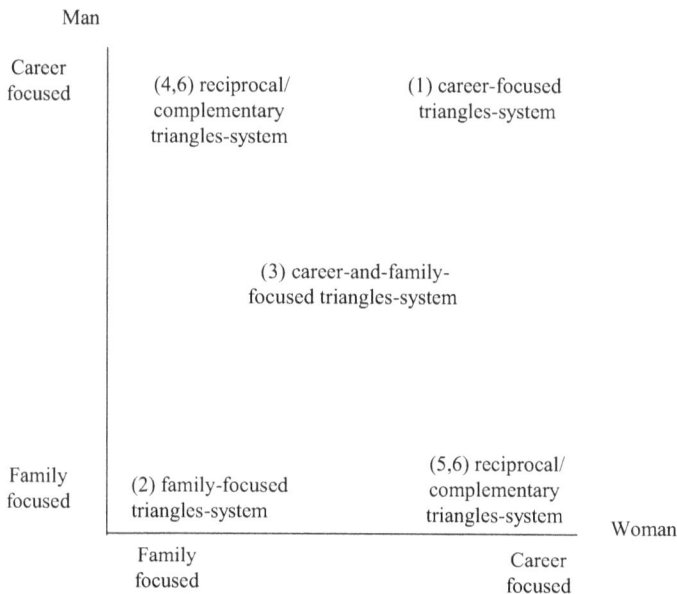

Figure 3.7: Continuum of couple work–family roles

in which the parents exchange complementary roles – sometimes the man is career focused and sometimes the woman is career focused. The place of each work–family triangles system is determined by analyzing the involvement, investment, and identity (Greenhaus & Powell, 2017) of the man and woman based on their perceptions.

Traditional gender roles, in terms of the behaviors expected for members of each sex, position the work–family triangles systems in the second quarter – work–family role type 4 – wherein the man is career focused and the woman is family focused. The man is the breadwinner of the family, whereas the woman is expected to be loving, nurturing, homemaking, and submissive.

Women in these triangles talked about sacrificing their career development. Some said they chose this setting because they believe this is the right way to raise kids. Others said that this setting is right for them, but they can understand and respect women who think otherwise. Many women said that they knew from the beginning of their relationship that their husband was work oriented and accepted it and its consequences. When this solution was synchronized between the members of the couple, the tension was low.

As noted, work–family role refers to parents' perceptions of the place each sphere has in their life. It accounts for involvement in the spheres, investment, and sense of identity (Greenhaus & Powell, 2017). When talking with parents about their and their spouse's work and family roles, they initially talked about involvement and investment of time. This was found to be the easiest and most quantifiable means of defining a parent as career focused or family focused. However, later, when the conversation became more profound, we understood that the role has other important meanings: emotional involvement and the personal identity. A parent who is career focused in terms of involvement and time investment but is emotionally family focused will remember that his child has an important test and will ask how the test went. When this parent sees something in the store his daughter talked about a month ago, the parent might buy it for her. A good example is the case of Jack.

> Jack is a senior high-tech man who spent many hours working and abroad but was emotionally involved in his family and developed good relationships with the children. In one case, when his son had an important contest abroad, he flew to the location and surprised him on the playing field.

A different case is that of Samuel, who was career focused in terms of involvement, time investment, and emotion.

> Samuel did not call his wife who just had an abortion. She completely understood why he could not come and be with her. She accepted it, but the loneliness of being emotionally alone with the situation was too much for her, and she could not forget it. Speaking with her 15 years after the event, it was still an emotional issue.

The distinction between physical and emotional involvement is important because we found that couples sometimes interpret lack of physical involvement as a lack of emotional involvement, and this harms the relationship. Awareness of the importance of expressing emotional involvement can help decrease couple tension and build a better understanding. The emotional axis in the work–family triaxial contract, elaborated in Chapter 6, addresses this unsynchronized element.

The work–family role type is the high-level way the couple decides to handle work and family needs and abilities. Each work–family role type is translated into lower-level decisions, managing the work–family role type. This depends on how the couple perceives the work and family needs and abilities. Here, we describe some examples of couples' perceptions and decisions as they manage the work–family role type.

Couples with a career-focused triangles system can perceive work and family needs and abilities differently and therefore, decide differently on managing their career-focused triangles system. We found four types of career-focused triangles system management. In the first, a large portion of childcare is provided by grandparents and nannies and not by the parents. The second type is couples that decide they do not want "our children to be raised by others" (as they say). There is considerable tension between them and their managers surrounding their request to spend time with their children without this affecting their career advancement. Other couples decide not to have children, because they think that they should not have children when both parents are career focused. The fourth kind of couples divide the weekdays: Every day, one parent, although still work focused, handles the children and family needs, allowing the other to be fully career focused and dedicated to work without family interference.

These examples show that each couple in a career-focused triangles system decides differently how to manage work and family needs and abilities. If the members of the couple were synchronized, the couple's tension was low. When the couple was not synchronized, the interpersonal relationship paid the price.

Most couples are synchronized regarding the triangles system work–family role but are not synchronized regarding the meaning, and particularly the extent, of the work–family role. This unsynchronized area can result in a considerable amount of tension and fights. An example is a case in which the man had a very successful business. He and his wife were synchronized on a complementary triangles system wherein he was career focused and she was family focused. The problem was that they perceived the complementary triangles system differently.

> Carter worked late hours, coming home at 22:00, and working on weekends to preserve and expand the business. Nora accepted the psychological contract that she alone handles all the family needs (home and children), but not that their marital relationship should be harmed. She felt like a single parent without a husband and that she had signed up only for the first part. Carter said he knows that when he wants to "come back," there will be no one there waiting for him. Nora developed a fulfilled life of her own. He was redundant.

In another case, the couple was synchronized regarding the triangles system work–family role but not synchronized regarding the meaning.

Owen and Aria agreed that Aria would be family oriented. However, Owen thought Aria should work part-time, whereas Aria wanted to be free and available for the children all day. Owen repeatedly emphasized that this was good for neither the kids nor their economic situation. He feared that when the children became older, it would be hard or even impossible for Owen to return to her career.

Summarizing the work–family roles segment of the couple work–family psychological contract, the couple has to decide on the work–family roles that match their personal, relational, family, and work needs. They have to synchronize the meaning of the work–family roles they choose and the way they decide to manage them.

The Manager–Employee's Spouse Dyad

Figure 3.8 illustrates the manager–employee's spouse dyad. This is an important dyad that affects the work-family triangle system. However, it does not get enough recognition in the academic field nor the consultation field. A notable exception is Perlow (1998), who studied spouses' reactions to the work demands of the employees and found that they strongly affect how employees respond to boundary control.

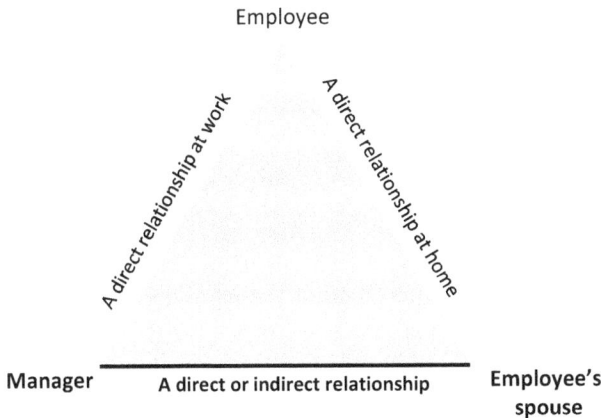

Figure 3.8: The Manager–Employee's Spouse Dyad.

Moreover, as we found, because managers' awareness of the importance of this dyad is very low, it is not appropriately managed. We found that the employee's spouse frequently has an important and powerful influence on the employee and the way he or she manages the dyad with the manager at work; for example, spouses can influence the extent to which the employees devote themselves to work, spouses can calm or incite the employee regarding the manager, and spouses can convince their spouse (the employee) to leave the workplace.

Spouses who were aware of their power said they were afraid they would influence their partner to engage in a major confrontation with the manager and therefore, attempted to manage their influence and be less involved.

> Mateo, who was involved in his wife's intensive relationship with her manager, expressed the significant influence of the spouse, stating: "When you marry a person, you marry his family. The same goes here. When you recruit an employee, in some sense, you recruit his family and his spouse as an important representative of the family."

The relationship between the manager and the employee's spouse can be direct or indirect. By direct, we mean that the manager and the spouse know each other directly and speak to each other. For example, when military families live on a military base, it is common for the manager (the commander) to know the spouses of the officers, meet them, and speak to them routinely. Direct dyads were also found wherein the manager and employee worked together for years and the manager met the spouse at various events, and in cases in which the manager thought it important to meet and know the spouse, created get-togethers. A unique case was that of David:

> David is a manager who routinely invites each employee and his or her spouse to a restaurant with his own wife (the manager's spouse), creating an out-of-office situation that enables an open conversation. David learns much from these events, and he recommended to some of his colleagues that they do the same. One, a religious manager, adopted the idea and started his own ritual, inviting employees and their family to Kabbalat Shabbat with his own family.

Another case is that of Grace, a manager of a small company we met while consulting:

> Grace thought it important that she get to know the spouses of her employees and vice versa. Once a year, she invites all employees with their spouses to a half-day workshop. Interviewing the spouses, we heard that these get-togethers were important and helped them "put a face to the person" they hear a lot about at home.

Most managers learn about the spouse indirectly from the employee. Depending on the work–family mixture, the manager might talk to the employee about family matters, learning about family needs and abilities. If these conversations are open and sincere, managers can learn what the spouse thinks about them as managers.

Whether the relationship is direct or indirect, the main point is the extent to which the manager knows and takes into consideration the spouse when thinking about or making a decision regarding or affecting the employee. Taking into consideration means bearing in mind that another important stakeholder is influenced by and influences the work dyad, the employee's spouse. Accounting for this other interest is part of a trusting relationship (concern), elaborated in Chapter 7. In the manager–spouse dyad, we give special attention to the extent to which the manager is aware of the spouse, because we found that the spouse is always aware of the manager's power and role in the employee's life.

The length of manager–spouse dyad, the triangle side, indicates the relationship quality. When the manager–spouse dyad side is short, it means that the relationship between the manager and the spouse is good. They know and appreciate one another, directly or indirectly. When the dyad side is long, the relationship is at a distance; they do not know or do not appreciate one another.

From practitioners' experience, there are two motivations for the manager to manage this dyad and ensure that the distance is short. The first motivation is humanistic, as demonstrated by the following quotes. A spouse noted:

> It was very important for me when the manager of Alon [her husband] called me on our anniversary, thanked me, acknowledging my role, and gave us a weekend in a hotel.

One senior manager in a big corporate, explained this motivation. He stated:

> I know my employees' spouses and if I know one of them has couple difficulties, I will not throw on him a complicated and demanding project that will make things worse.

Conversely, in a case wherein the manager didn't believe he has to manage his dyad with his employees' spouses, one of his employees mentioned:

> My boss doesn't care about my family. I am very frustrated. It is as if I am only good as an employee.

In the same line of thought, another employee in a different company but with the same type of manager told us:

> When my daughter was born, my boss didn't send anything to my wife, didn't ask if we need something. He ignored the event. That was when I understood he really doesn't care.

These quotes demonstrate that the spouse is an important person for the employee and should be seen as person and not as a means to an end or non-relevant.

The second motivation to manage the manager–spouse dyad is cost analysis or utilitarian. The spouse, as shown in the following examples, has an important role in the employee's life, and so it is cost effective to know (directly or indirectly) and take the spouse into consideration when managing the employee. Emilia, a manager told us:

> If I ask Ellie [the employee] to work on Friday, Jackson [her spouse] won't like it and I will feel it on Sunday and Monday. If I want Ellie to function at her best, I need Jackson to be supportive.

Another case that demonstrates the worth of managing the manager–spouse dyad is that of Lillian, a manager in a delivery company.

> Lillian learned from one of her employees, Stella, that her husband was incredibly angry about the work terms. She offered a meeting to talk about the terms. In the meeting, she discovered that both Stella and her spouse didn't fully understand the terms and after explaining it and updating some of the things in a way that better suited them, things calmed down and Lillian felt that Stella was more committed.

In another case, Hannah, a manager, consulted with us regarding a role she wanted to offer one of her employees, Zoe.

> Stella is leaving and I want Zoe to replace her, but it means a lot of business trips and she has little children and her husband is a workaholic. I know it will be hard for her. I learned from many conversations with Zoe that she respects her husband's opinion and that he always encourages her to develop her career. I think that when I offer her the role, I should emphasize its potential to promote her career, so when she consults with him, he will encourage her to accept it even though it means many flights. I hope that way she will get his blessing and his help with the children.

Matthew, a manager in a high-tech company, emphasized the idea of reciprocity:

> If I show my employees that I do care about them and their spouse, I build their commitment, and when I need their spouse to be there for the company, I feel they are. It's a two-way street. You have to give so you will get.

Another example of the cost analysis or economic motive to manage the manager–spouse dyad is the case of Lucy, an employee in a very demanding job, who told us:

> My husband respects and appreciates my manager, so when I come home late or work on the weekend, he sees it favorably. In my previous job, it was the opposite. He despised my manager and didn't understand why I invested in the work.

Violet, a spouse in another triangle in the same company, expanded on that point:

> My place in the triangle is assured. His [the manager's] is not. If he is clever, he will make sure I like him and want my husband to continue working for him.

It may seem that the more the manager knows about and considers the spouse's needs and abilities, the better it will be. Nevertheless, a too-tight dyad was perceived as not appropriate and invasive. Practitioners' experience shows that the relationship between the manager and the spouse can be described as a diagram of three relationship-intensity spaces, as shown in Figure 3.9. The stars represent mismanagement of the dyad by the manager, whereas the dots represent effective dyad management. The three spaces in the figure describe three relationship frameworks: invasiveness, involvement, and disengagement.

An invasive dyad is one in which the manager makes decisions for the couple, as when a military commander told his officer:

> You are not going out on this mission; it's dangerous, and your wife is pregnant.

An involvement dyad is one in which the manager takes an interest in the spouse, bears him or her in mind when managing the employee, and is considerate when possible. For example:

> I know that your wife has an important test; you can leave earlier this month to let her study.

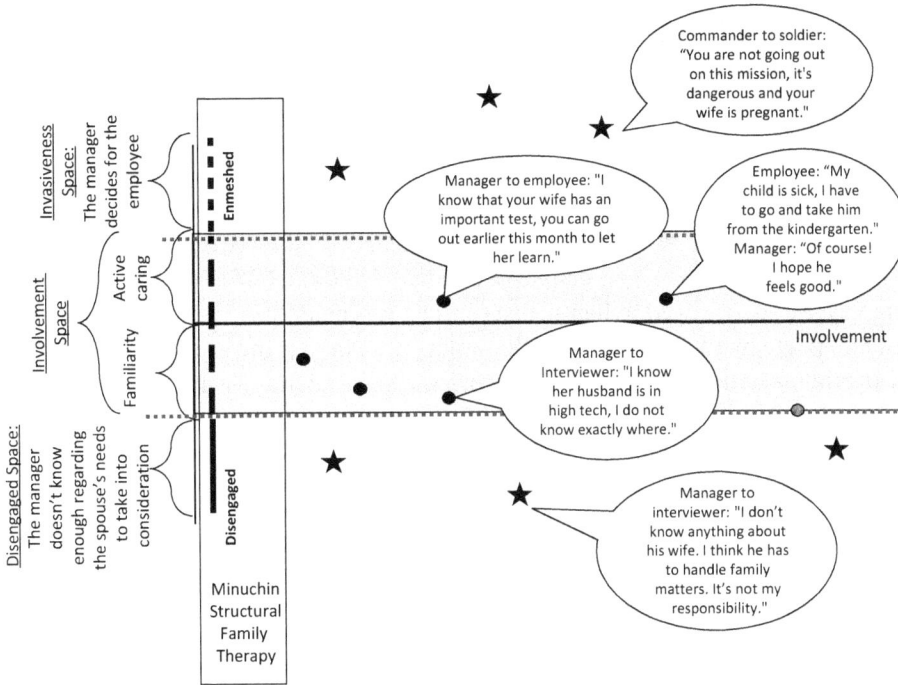

Figure 3.9: Relationship-intensity spaces of manager–employee's spouse dyad.

A disengaged dyad is one in which the manager ignores the spouse. As one manager told us:

> I manage the employee, and he manages his relationship with his spouse. I don't care how he does it, and I don't think I have to take it into account when managing him.

Our division (invasiveness, involvement, and disengagement) is based on the boundaries of the family relationship described by Minuchin (1974). A well-known and appreciated family therapist, Minuchin studied families and concluded that their boundaries are characterized along a continuum from enmeshment through semidiffuse permeability to rigidity. Functional families have semidiffuse boundaries, whereas dysfunctional families have enmeshed or rigid boundaries (Minuchin, 1974). Our experience in organizational dynamics is aligned with this argumentation. We found that triangle systems that keep the manager–spouse dyad in the involvement space enable a collaboration when managing the complex work–family fit, as explained later in the book.

Reciprocal Influence between the Work–Family Dyads' Psychological Contracts

The five dyads of the work–family triangles system are tied together. Every work–family triangles system has its work–family psychological contract. A contract has to account for the five dyads' work–family psychological contracts: (1) the man's manager–employee dyad, (2) the woman's manager–employee dyad, (3) the couple dyad, (4) the man's manager–employee's spouse dyad, and (5) the woman's manager–employee's spouse dyad. When such a contract is synchronized with all stakeholders and therefore, with all dyads, then the system can manage the work–family interface with minimal tension. Otherwise, we witness a powerful triangle dynamic that affects all dyads. Therefore, in Chapter 4, we elaborate on triangle dynamics in general, and then, we analyze the work–family triangle dynamic.

> **New Concepts in the Chapter**
> – *Work–family hierarchy* – One of the work–family psychological contract segments characterizing which sphere makes the rules and which sphere needs to adjust.
> – *Work–family mixture* – One of the work–family psychological contract segments characterizing the extent to and intensity with which the two spheres interrelate (a continuum from work–family separation through work–family interaction to work–family integration).
> – *Work–family role* – One of the work–family psychological contract segments characterizing the way a couple decides to divide family and work roles (each member can be career focused, family focused, or career-and-family focused).

WFTS Exercise

Triangle of Life

Practice for Couples

Design your couple work–family psychological contract using the following exercises. In the first stage, you will be asked to identify your current couple work–family psychological contract. Have an open dialogue regarding the way you, as a couple, operate the work–family interface today. At this point, do not assess whether you are satisfied with the psychological contract. Just find out how you think things are going at the moment. In the second stage, discuss the contract you want and how you want to manage the interface. Step by step, design the psychological contract you want. Some couples can carry out this process alone, whereas others will prefer to involve a professional who can help reveal the situation today and shape the contract they want. As a couple, see what is best for you.

Stage 1 – The current work–family psychological contract
Work–Family Role
Please mark how you currently manage the division of roles between you and your spouse:

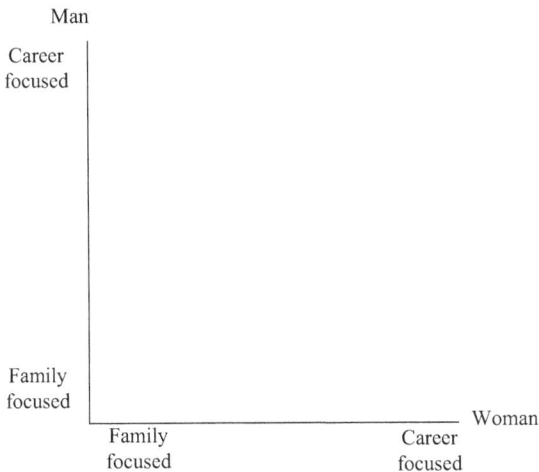

Explain your selection:

_____

_____

_____

Work–Family Hierarchy

Please mark how you currently manage the work–family hierarchy of your triangle system. Place points on the drawing that indicate the current balance regarding who adjusts to whom. Mark two points, one in relation to the work of the woman and the other in relation to the work of the man.

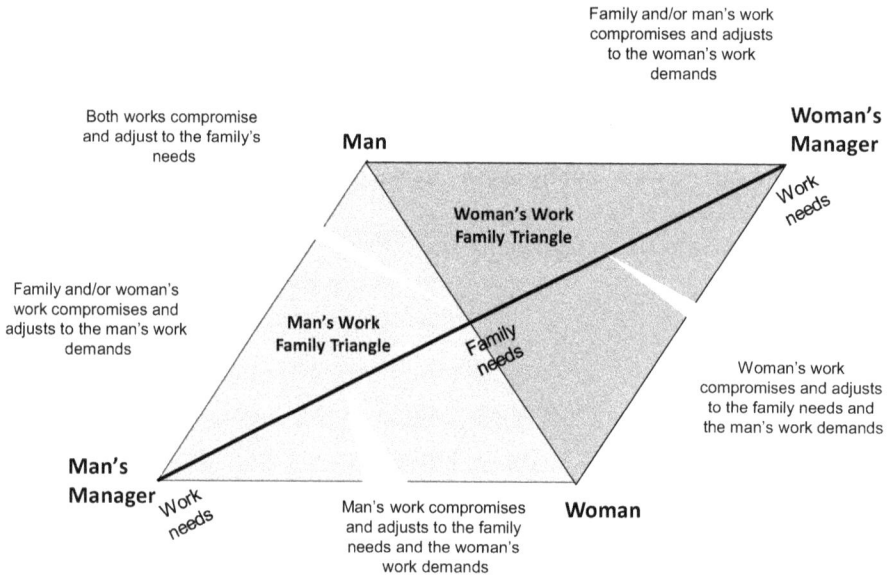

Family and/or man's work compromises and adjusts to the woman's work demands

Both works compromise and adjust to the family's needs

Man

Woman's Manager

Work needs

Woman's Work Family Triangle

Family and/or woman's work compromises and adjusts to the man's work demands

Man's Work Family Triangle

Family needs

Woman's work compromises and adjusts to the family needs and the man's work demands

Man's Manager

Work needs

Man's work compromises and adjusts to the family needs and the woman's work demands

Woman

Explain your selection:

_____

_____

_____

Work–Family Mixture

Please mark how you currently manage the interaction between work and family. Indicate the current location of the man's work–family mixture and for the woman's work–family mixture.

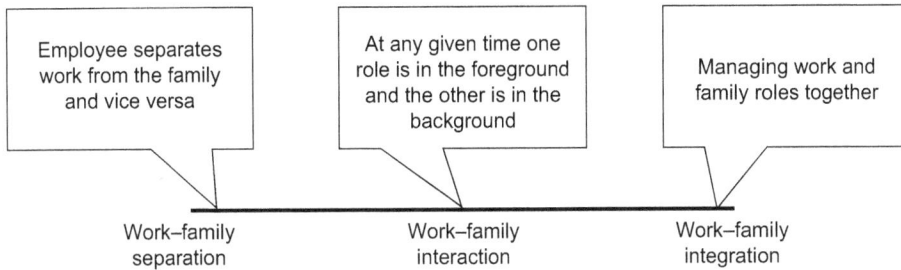

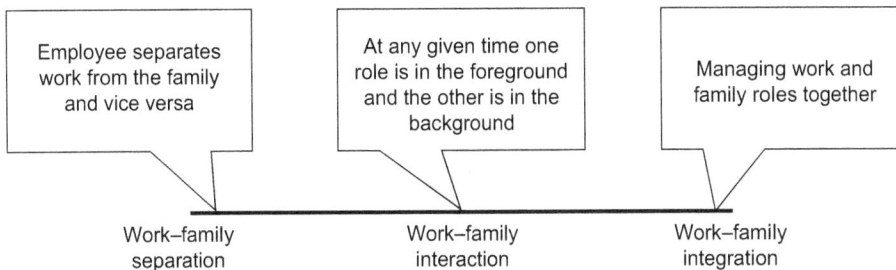

Man's work–family mixture:

| Employee separates work from the family and vice versa | At any given time one role is in the foreground and the other is in the background | Managing work and family roles together |

| Work–family separation | Work–family interaction | Work–family integration |

Explain your selection:

_____

_____

_____

Woman's work–family mixture:

| Employee separates work from the family and vice versa | At any given time one role is in the foreground and the other is in the background | Managing work and family roles together |

| Work–family separation | Work–family interaction | Work–family integration |

Explain your selection:

_____

_____

_____

Relationship-intensity spaces of manager–employee's spouse dyad

Please mark how the manager–employee's spouse dyad operates at present. Indicate the status of the man's manager–employee's spouse dyad and the woman's manager–employee's spouse dyad.

Man's manager–employee's spouse dyad:

Disengaged Space:
The manager doesn't know enough regarding the spouse's needs to take into consideration

Involvement Space

Familiarity

Active caring

Invasiveness Space:
The manager decides for the employee

Disengaged   Enmeshed

Explain your selection:

_____

_____

_____

Woman's manager–employee's spouse dyad:

Disengaged Space:
The manager doesn't know enough regarding the spouse's needs to take into consideration

Involvement Space

Familiarity

Active caring

Invasiveness Space:
The manager decides for the employee

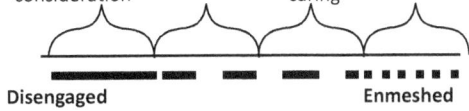

Disengaged

Enmeshed

Explain your selection:

_____

_____

_____

Stage 2 – Develop the desired work–family psychological contract
Work–Family Role

Please mark how you would prefer to manage the division of roles between you and your spouse:

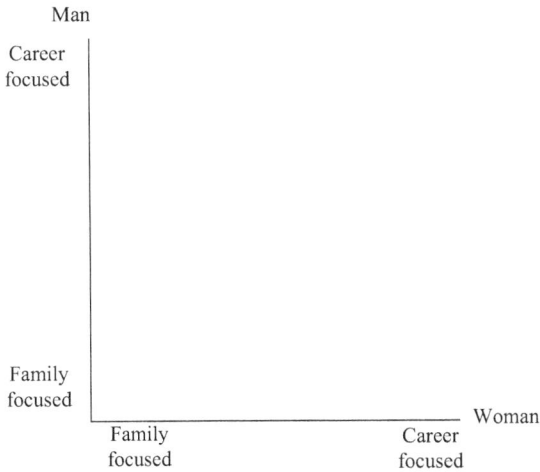

Man

Career focused

Family focused

Family focused

Career focused

Woman

Explain your choice:

_____

_____

_____

Work–Family Hierarchy

Please mark how you would prefer to manage the work–family hierarchy of your triangle system. Place points on the drawing that indicate the right balance for you regarding who adjusts to whom. Mark two points, one in relation to the work of the woman and the other in relation to the work of the man.

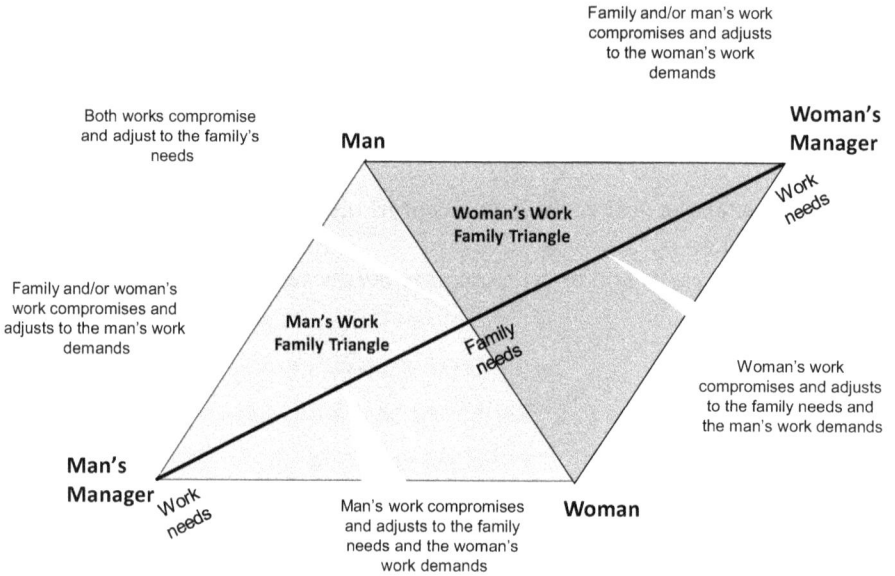

Family and/or man's work compromises and adjusts to the woman's work demands

Both works compromise and adjust to the family's needs

Man

Woman's Manager

Work needs

Woman's Work Family Triangle

Family and/or woman's work compromises and adjusts to the man's work demands

Man's Work Family Triangle

Family needs

Woman's work compromises and adjusts to the family needs and the man's work demands

Man's Manager

Work needs

Man's work compromises and adjusts to the family needs and the woman's work demands

Woman

Explain your choice:

_____

_____

_____

Work–Family Mixture

Please mark how you would prefer to manage the interaction between work and family. Indicate the right place for the man's work–family mixture and for the woman's work–family mixture.

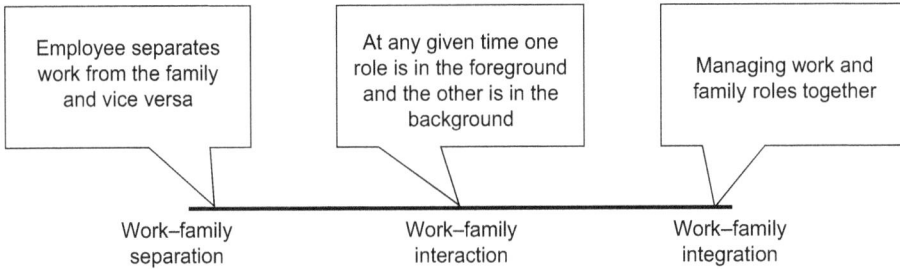

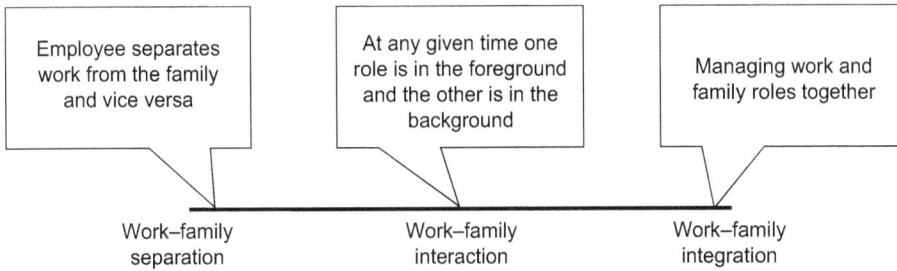

Man's work–family mixture:

Employee separates work from the family and vice versa	At any given time one role is in the foreground and the other is in the background	Managing work and family roles together

| Work–family separation | Work–family interaction | Work–family integration |

Explain your choice:

_____

_____

_____

Woman's work–family mixture:

Employee separates work from the family and vice versa	At any given time one role is in the foreground and the other is in the background	Managing work and family roles together

| Work–family separation | Work–family interaction | Work–family integration |

Explain your choice:

Relationship-intensity spaces of manager–employee's spouse dyad

Please mark how you would prefer that the manager–employee's spouse dyad be managed. Point the right place for the man's manager–employee's spouse dyad and for the woman's manager–employee's spouse dyad.

Man's manager–employee's spouse dyad:

Disengaged Space:
The manager doesn't know enough regarding the spouse's needs to take into consideration

Involvement Space

Invasiveness Space:
The manager decides for the employee

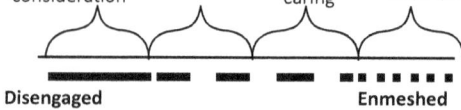

Familiarity

Active caring

Disengaged

Enmeshed

Explain your choice:

Woman's manager–employee's spouse dyad:

Disengaged Space:
The manager doesn't know enough regarding the spouse's needs to take into consideration

Involvement Space

Invasiveness Space:
The manager decides for the employee

Familiarity   Active caring

Disengaged   Enmeshed

Explain your choice:

_____

_____

_____

References

Baruch, Y., & Rousseau, D. M. (2019). Integrating psychological contracts and ecosystems in career studies and management. *Academy of Management Annals*, *13*(1), 84–111.

Becker, P. E., & Moen, P. (1999). Scaling back: Dual-earner couples' work-family strategies. *Journal of Marriage and the Family*, 995–1007.

Greenhaus, J. H., & Powell, G. N. (2017) *Making Work and Family Work: From hard choices to smart choices*. Routledge.

Han, S. K., & Moen, P. (1999). Work and family over time: A life course approach. *The Annals of the American Academy of Political and Social Science*, *562*(1), 98–110.

Huffman, A. H., Casper, W. J., & Payne, S. C. (2014). How does spouse career support relate to employee turnover? Work interfering with family and job satisfaction as mediators. *Journal of Organizational Behavior*, *35*(2), 194–212.

Marks, S. R., & MacDermid, S. M. (1996). Multiple roles and the self: A theory of role balance. *Journal of Marriage and the Family*, 417–432.

Minuchin, S. (1974). *Families and Family Therapy*. Cambridge, MA: Harvard Univ.

Moen, P. (2003). *It's about time: Couples and careers*. Cornell University Press.

Moen, P., & Wethington, E. (1992). The concept of family adaptive strategies. Annual review of sociology, 233–251.

Moen, P., & Yu, Y. (2000). Effective work/life strategies: Working couples, work conditions, gender, and life quality. *Social problems*, *47*(3), 291–326.

Perlow LA (1998) Boundary control: The social ordering of work and family time in a high-tech corporation. *Administrative Science Quarterly* 43(2): 328–357.

Pittman, J. F., & Blanchard, D. (1996). The effects of work history and timing of marriage on the division of household labor: A life-course perspective. *Journal of Marriage and the Family*, 78–90.

Robinson, S. L., & Rousseau, D. M. (1994). Violating the psychological contract: Not the exception but the norm. *Journal of organizational behavior*, *15*(3), 245–259.

Rousseau, D. M. (1989). Psychological and implied contracts in organizations. *Employee responsibilities and rights journal*, *2*(2), 121–139.

Turnley, W. H., & Feldman, D. C. (2000). Re-examining the effects of psychological contract violations: unmet expectations and job dissatisfaction as mediators. Journal of organizational behavior, 21(1), 25–42.

Chapter 4
Triangling: The Triad Work–Family Relationship

> Energy is contagious, positive and negative alike. I will forever be mindful of what and
> who I am allowing into my space.
> – Alex Elle

The work–family triangle system is the space where the work–family interface takes place. The structure of a triangle features three people and the relationship spaces between them. As Alix Elle wrote, the energy of this space is determined by its three players, whether positive or negative. In the previous chapter, we examined the relationship of the three dyads in this space. In the current chapter, we explore the triad relationship. The dynamics of this interplay result in the emotional climate of work and family space, the degree of tension and anxiety among the three players, and the space among them. Before we explore how the players generate this energy in the work and family fields, we elaborate on how a triangle relationship works in general.

A Triangle Relationship

A relationship, in general, refers to the way in which two or more people feel and behave toward each other – their connection and involvement. A triangle relationship is a relationship among three people. To be precise, a triangle relationship is the interaction of three dyad relationships. This interaction stabilizes the dyads because it enables each dyad to involve the third person when it cannot tolerate the tension in the dyad. Bowen described triangles as the smallest stable relationship unit (Kerr & Bowen, 1988). This is called "*triangling*," when the inevitable anxiety in a dyad is relieved by involving a vulnerable third party who either takes sides or provides a detour for the anxiety (Guerin et al., 1996; James, 1989). Thus, in a triangle, the tension can shift around three relationships and therefore, it can tolerate more tension. Bowen chose the term triangling to convey that this concept has a specific meaning beyond that implied by "triad" (Bowen, 1985).

Bowen (1966) observed cycles of closeness and distance of the emotional involvement among the players. This emotional involvement is represented by the side length. Emotional involvement means the level of involvement, communication, and concern on a continuum. At one extreme are highly permeable interpersonal boundaries in which there is a denial of differences and a high level of involvement, communication, and concern. At the disengaged end of the continuum is an extreme lack of responsiveness and underinvolvement of members with one another. Fogarty (1976), a student of Bowen, maintained that all people seek closeness and that to maintain that closeness and still handle anxiety, they form a triangle. Therefore, to stabilize a relationship,

https://doi.org/10.1515/9783110759808-004

the dyad must involve a third party to help maintain its closeness. The third person assumes an outside position. In periods of stress, the outside position is the most comfortable and desired position. The inside position is plagued by anxiety, along with its emotional closeness. The outsider serves to preserve the inside couple's relationship. Paradoxically, a triangle is more stable than a dyad, but a triangle creates an odd man out, which is a very difficult position for individuals to tolerate. Anxiety generated by expecting to be or serving as the odd man out is a potent force in triangles.

Fogarty (1975) focused on the relationship movement of each individual. People have three movement options in a relationship: They can move toward the other person, they can move away, or they can stand still. The movement is driven by an increase in the level of emotional arousal of the individual and their emotional response (emotional reactivity) to the behavior of the other person or their perception of the other person's emotional state. Emotional arousal in the individual, together with the reactive movement it drives, is the fuel that feeds the activation of triangles. Emotional reactivity is the key to seeing how unstable dyads produce triangles. Each movement serves to calm their emotional state and make the environment as emotionally safe as possible.

One way to understand triangle dynamics is to use Fogarty's (1975) notion of a rubber band holding three people together. Imagine three people with a rubber band around them. They have to keep the rubber band taut (perhaps by an unspoken but unbreakable rule). In this situation, a change in the position of one will necessarily create a change in the position of the others or an increased tension between them. The rubber band (closed system) keeps the sum of the distances among the three people constant. If one moves away, the other two will pull closer to each other. This closed system, this rubber band effect, keeps the system from breaking but is also very limiting. Maintaining the rubber band so that it does not snap or fall to the floor is a reactive process, the necessary tension that requires each individual in the triangle to keep the focus on where the other two people are and what they are doing. Each individual must move in reaction to the moves of the other two and cannot move freely in reaction to self. The consequence (i.e., function) of this structure and the accompanying process of the triangle is that the three relationships are stabilized and change is prevented.

Under calm conditions, it is difficult to identify triangles, but they emerge clearly under stress. Bowen did not suggest that the process of triangling was necessarily dysfunctional (Brown, 1999), but viewed it as a useful way of grasping the notion that original tension is acted out elsewhere. A third party's involvement distracts the members of a dyad from resolving their relationship impasse. When a third party is drawn in, the focus shifts to criticizing or worrying about the new outsider, which in turn, prevents the original complainants from resolving their tension (Guerin et al., 1996).

Triangulation can be a way to stabilize the emotional state and make the environment as emotionally safe as possible. It can be a constructive process when a person attempts to control the flow, interpretation, and nuances of communication between two actors, ensuring communication flows and constantly relating back to them. Examples include a parent attempting to control communication between two children or a relationship partner attempting to control communication between the other partner and the other partner's friends, family, or colleagues at work. But it can also be a destructive and destabilizing the emotional state. It can polarize relations and escalate conflict. Figure 4.1 describes the triangling process.

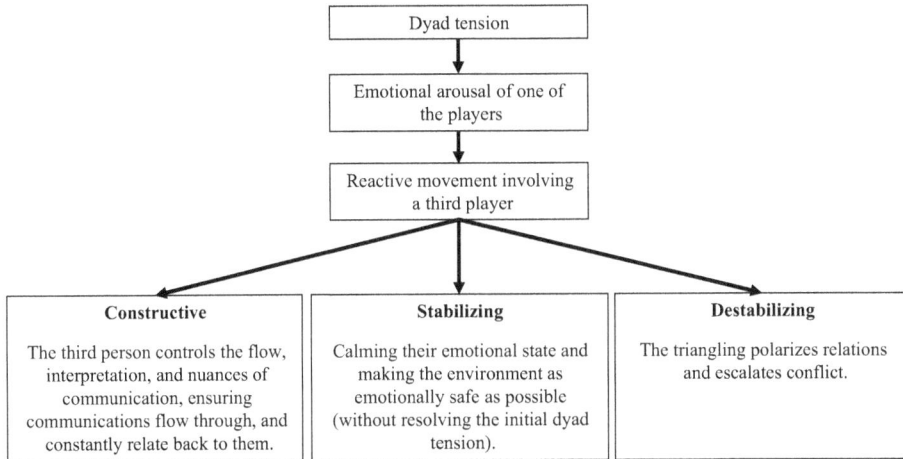

Figure 4.1: Triangling process.

Fixed Roles Created by Cycles of Closeness and Distance

In a triangle, cycles of closeness and distance repeat themselves and thus, people come to have fixed roles in relation to each other (Bowen, 1976). The well-known example of this is the father–mother–child triangle. The mother gets close to her child, resulting in moving away from the father. He is the outsider in the triangle. With time, he comes to have the characteristics of passive and distant, getting close to his work – a role of a breadwinner. The mother gets into the dominant and caregiving role. If there is tension in the couple relationship, the mother gets closer to the child, intensifying her dominant caregiving role and moving away from the father, her husband. Figure 4.2 depicts this kind of triangle relationship.

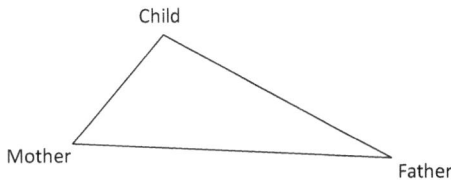

Figure 4.2: Unhealthy father–mother–child triangle.

Let's assume that they go to family therapy and design together a triangle they think is suitable for them. The mother gets closer to the father, creating a strong couple relationship, and a little further away from her the child, changing the enmeshed relationship with a healthy separated mother–child relationship. In this case, the father can move a little bit toward to the child and create a healthier triangle, as illustrated in Figure 4.3. In this triangle, the roles change. The husband has the role of an involved father and not only a breadwinner, and the mother develops another role and not only a caregiver.

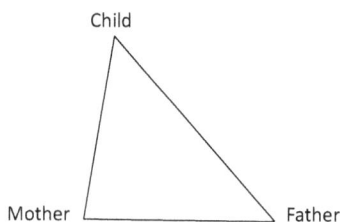

Child

Mother   Father

Figure 4.3: Healthy father–mother–child triangle.

Triangulation, and the fixed roles derived from it, is widely recognized as a stabilizing factor in a family, at work, among social groups, and other contexts. We all engage in triangulation because triangles help us cope when we are struggling with another person. Work–family conflict is a rich platform for triangling.

Triangling in the Work–Family Interface

Driven by Bowen's triangling, but not restricting ourselves to it, we examined many *work–family trianglings (WFT)*. Figure 4.4 summarizes all forms of work–family triangling. The triangling can be triggered by a tensioned dyad, as in Bowen's triangling, or by a desirable dyad, which one of the players is interested in strengthening. We start by exploring cases where a dyad with unstable tension triggered the movement of the triangle. This can be triggered by each of the three dyads: couple dyad, work dyad, or manager–spouse dyad. The work–family triangling will be different for each trigger.

As an example of tension in the couple dyad, we can think of a woman who feels uncomfortable with too much closeness to her husband. She may begin to withdraw, perhaps toward another activity such as work (the third point of the triangle). The man then pursues the woman, which results in increased withdrawal to the initial triangled-in activity (the work), and the person (the manager). The triangling in this case intensifies the couple's tension. In a different scenario, the man accepts the new distance in their couple dyad and does not pursue her. This triangling prevents resolution of the couple's tension but does not intensify it. The case of Isaac started as intensified tension and ended in a resolved conflict.

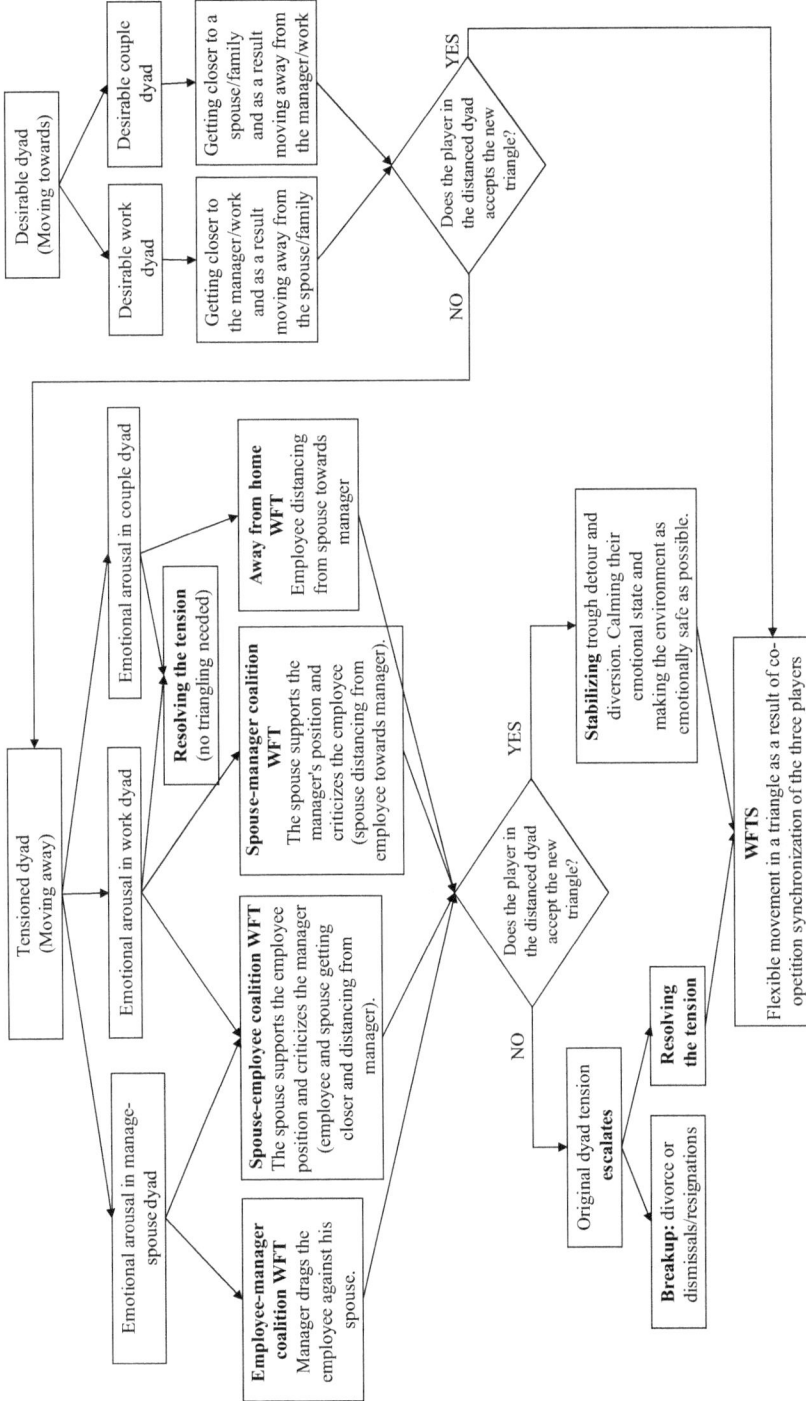

Figure 4.4: Work–family triangling forms.

There was considerable tension in the couple relationship, and Isaac began staying long hours at the office and returning home late to distance himself from his wife (the members of the couple dyad moved further away from each other, whereas those of the work dyad became closer). His wife complained about the long hours he spends in the office, returning home when she and the child are already asleep. The more she complained and the couple had many ugly fights, the more the tension increased. Isaac stayed even longer at the office, until his wife said she wants a divorce. They decided to go to couples therapy.

When their relationship got better, the couple dyad got closer on account of the work dyad. They didn't need to bypass the tension and avoid resolving it anymore. We learned about this case from Isaac's colleague, who explained:

"I must say I have ambivalent feeling regarding Isaac. I am happy he solved things with his wife. They have three young children, and they were close to divorcing each other. But the one that pays the price is me. I got used to it that he leaves last, volunteers to fly to clients, and now, he reduced his flights and I have to take them. When problems stay open at the end of the day, I am the one that has to close them. I am single, so everyone at the office feels it's OK."

Figure 4.5 shows the triangling movement in Isaac's case. Note that the perimeter of the triangle does not change, only the length of the sides varies.

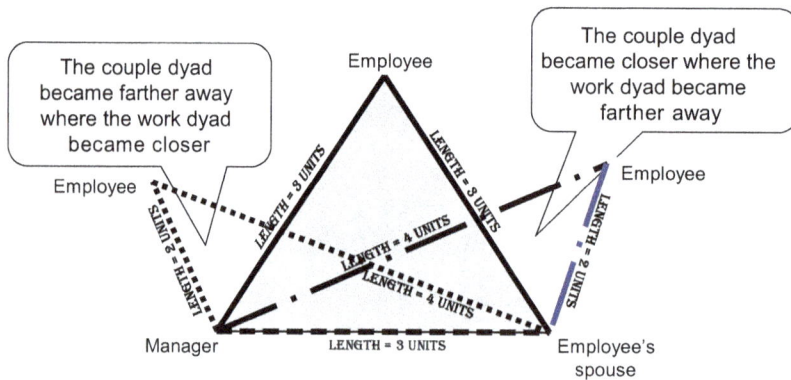

Figure 4.5: Isaac's WFT.

As we see, through a process of getting the work dyad members closer on account of distancing the couple dyad, the couple tension can be intensified or stabilized through avoidance. Intensifying can challenge the couple relationship to appoint of breakup or resolution of the initial conflict.

When the triangling is triggered by a tensioned work dyad, we found that most of the time, the spouse supports the employee and together they think of the correct way to respond. This moves their dyad closer and distances the work dyad. As in the case of triangling due to couple dyad tension, this "coalition triangling" can stabilize the triangle, intensify the tension, or eventually resolve it.

This triangle movement, where the couple dyad moves closer at the expense of the work dyad, can be a movement that is synchronized between all stakeholders and not a couple coalition triggered by tension in the work dyad. An example is the case mentioned in Chapter 3, where the spouse had an important test and the manager gave the employee a very flexible month to enable him to be at home more so his spouse could study. In synchronized triangling, the outcome distance in the work dyad is not a means to bypass a dyad tension but a synchronized path to manage a conflict. This way, the solution, even if it seems the same solution, it is a healthy one because it is managed and not reactive; it is a conscious choice made by three stakeholders. No high tension is involved, and we don't witness stress symptoms.

Another synchronized triangle movement case occurs during "deadlines," times in many triangles when the employee has to be at the office at all hours for a short period. If the stakeholders are synchronized regarding the understanding that in times of stress, the work dyad becomes closer at the expense of the couple dyad, there won't be couple tension that will trigger a tensioned triangling, and the triangling can be synchronized and managed without adding stress to the already stressful situation. A triangle psychological contract that enables flexible triangle movement is a *"co-operation WFTS psychological contract,"* which is elaborated in Chapter 5 on work–family triangle synchronization.

Another interesting type of triangle movement is illustrated in Figure 4.6. In this triangle movement, the trigger of the movement is the manager–spouse dyad. There is tension in the manager–spouse dyad because the spouse is angry about the manager's behavior toward the employee. The manager–spouse dyad becomes further away, meaning the manager–spouse's side lengthened (marked as 1 in the figure).

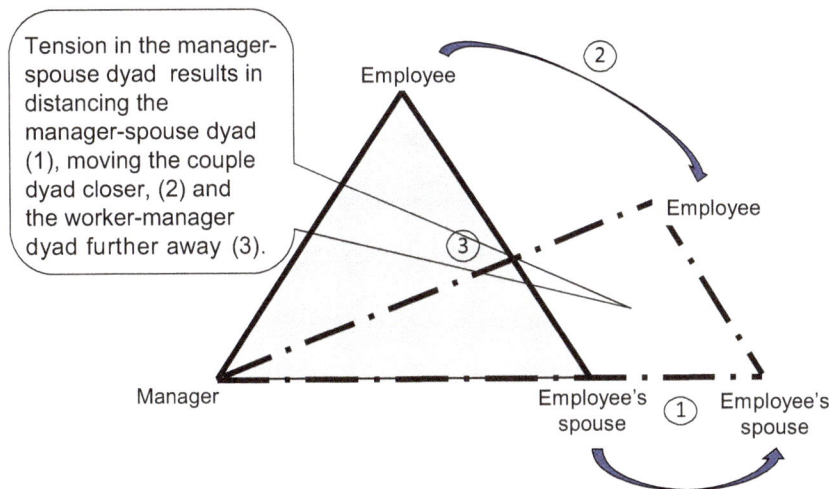

Figure 4.6: Employee–spouse coalition WFT.

The spouse incites the employee against his manager, resulting in bringing the couple dyad closer (marked as 2 in the figure) and pushing the employee–manager dyad further apart (marked as 3 in the figure).

The opposite dynamic pattern occurs when the reason for the tension is the manager's bitterness with the spouse. This triangle movement is illustrated in Figure 4.7, demonstrating a case where the spouse prevented the employee from accepting a promotion.

> Mila, an officer in the army, offered Chloe, her employee, a promotion. Chloe's spouse, John, did not want her to take the promotion. He wanted her to give priority to their dyad and be committed to the family. A year prior, she had been offered another promotion and rejected it because of John's influence. This time Mila did not yield. She believed Chloe should accept the promotion. She was angry with John for preventing his wife's advancement. She offered to speak with him, but Chloe asked her not to do so, saying that it would only make matters worse.

In this case, the unsynchronized work–family hierarchy, noted in Chapter 3, among the three stakeholders created considerable tension between all three dyads. The manager was angry with the spouse, distancing the manager–spouse dyad (marked as 1 in the figure). The manager tried to influence the employee against the spouse's agenda. This resulted in distancing the employee from his spouse (marked as 2 in the figure) and brought the work dyad closer (marked as 3 in the figure).

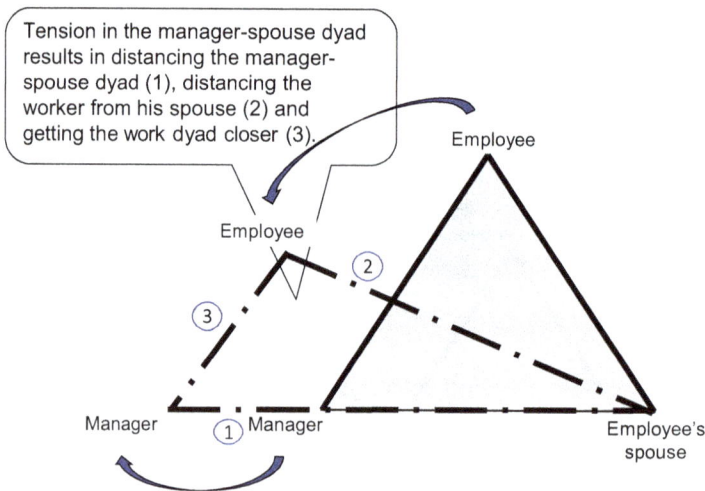

> Tension in the manager-spouse dyad results in distancing the manager-spouse dyad (1), distancing the worker from his spouse (2) and getting the work dyad closer (3).

Figure 4.7: Employee–manager coalition WFT.

A unique case of dyadic movement was the case of Luna and Luke, where the manager–spouse dyad moved closer at the expense of both the work and couple dyads.

Aria (Samuel's spouse) agreed with Dylan (Samuel's manager) and "took his side" regarding the way Samuel behaved in a delicate matter. The work dyad tension became couple tension, resulting in a greater distance in both dyads, the work dyad and couple dyad, as illustrated in Figure 4.8.

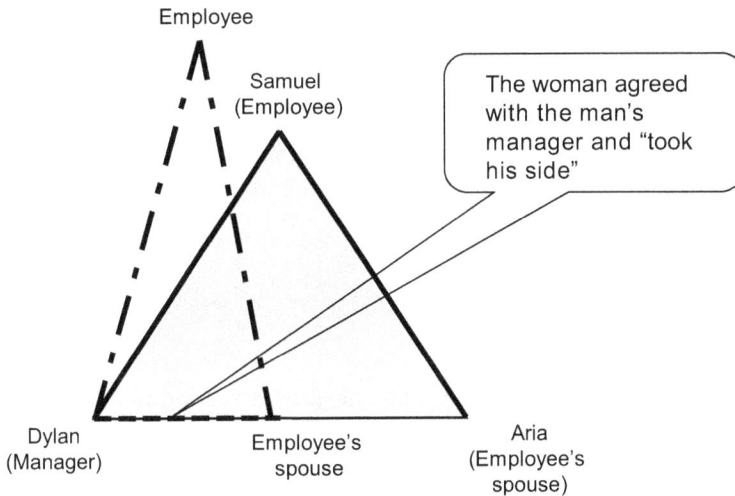

Figure 4.8: Spouse–manager coalition WFT.

In a similar situation, where the spouse saw eye to eye with the manager, there was no movement in the triangle.

> Micah (Layla's spouse) agreed with Layla's manager regarding the way Layla behaved in a delicate matter. Micah told us he decided to be on Layla's side, although he thought she was wrong, for the sake of their relationship. There was no movement in the triangle.

These examples demonstrate again the influence of the spouse on the work dyad, and therefore, the reason the work–family interface should be managed as a triangle system.

Triangulation and Fixed Roles in Work–Family Triangles

As we noted, triangulation creates fixed roles. The same process can happen in the work–family triangle. The triangling process of repetitive pattern creates work–family roles. Triangles can drag employees into a "workaholic" role, avoiding home involvement and responsibilities. In these cases, spouses can be dragged to an "unsupporting" role, nagging the employee to come home. Instead of resolving conflicts, the roles become rigid and the player in each role becomes extreme in their role. The triangle of Emma, Carter, and Emma's manager demonstrates this dynamic.

Emma and Carter were not synchronized regarding their work–family mixture. Emma was a deputy director of education in a prestigious high school and thought they should practice work–family integration. She works all day, talking to teachers and parents while she is involved in family matters. Carter worked in a food factory wanted the work–family mixture to be work–family separation. When he came home at 18:00, he wanted them both to be free from work, spending the evening with each other and with their children. He got frustrated every time she answered a phone call or an email from work in the middle of their conversation or a game with the kids. They had many fights regarding the issue, but never solved it. He criticized her, saying "You are a bad mother, and your work is more important to you than our family." He always added: "Your manager is a feminist and tries to change the world at our expense." Emma, in return, criticized him for not supporting her and preferring that she leaves work to stay at home and take care of him and the children. With time, it got worse, and they could not see a way out of their triangle roles.

Triangle Maze

If the tension is too high for the triangle to contain, it spreads to a series of triangles, adding another stakeholder. It can spread to a triangle of the couple with the mother-in-law, a triangle of manager–employee–manager's manager, or any other player who is brought into the situation to reduce tension. It is important to emphasize that spreading the tension, both from two-person system to three-person system or from a triangle to a series of triangles, can stabilize a system or escalate the tension. Either way, it does not resolve it. From this perspective, we can see life not so much as a series of paths to be chosen, but as a maze of triangle shoals and reefs to be navigated. Bowen (1985), Fogarty (1975), Haley (1987), and Minuchin (1974) considered it significant that people frequently organize their interior lives and relationship lives in threes. Figure 4.9 demonstrates an example of a work–family triangle maze.

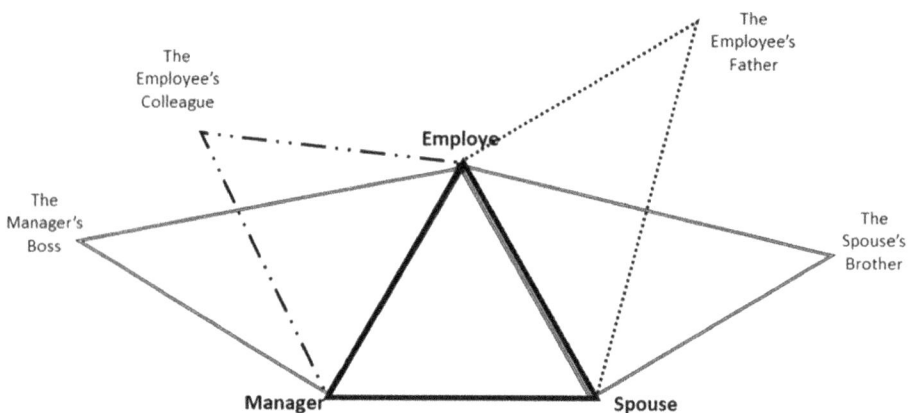

Figure 4.9: Work–family triangle maze.

In dual-earner families, there is a structural triangles maze, the work–family triangles system. This system, illustrated in Figure 4.10, is composed of the woman's work–family triangle and the man's work–family triangle.

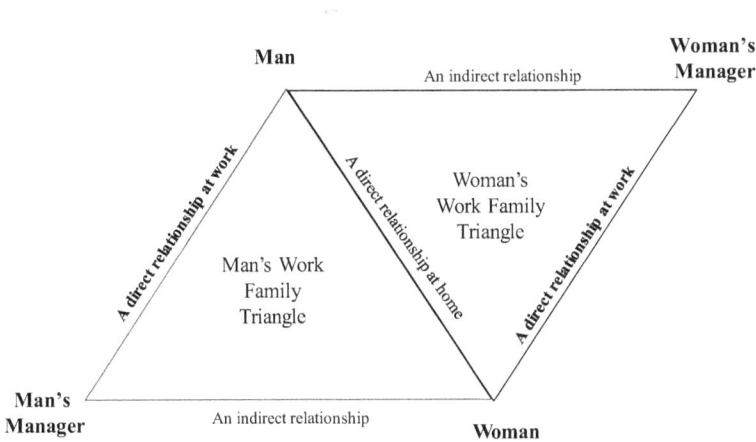

Figure 4.10: Work–family triangles system.

A common case of a work–family triangles system that stabilizes a couple tension can be seen in Figure 4.11. In this maze, the couple withdraws from each other toward their work to avoid the tension.

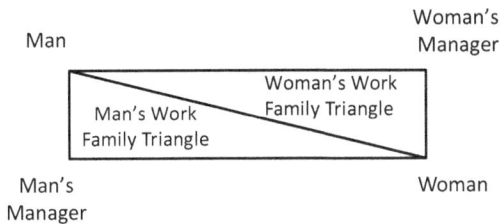

Figure 4.11: Work–family triangles system stabilizing couple's tension.

The case of Jane and Ben, illustrated in Figure 4.12, is another example of a work–family triangles system stabilizing function.

As a result of a conflict regarding Ben's performance with an important client, the relationship between Ben and his manager became saturated with tension. When the tension increased and overwhelmed Ben, he distanced himself from his manager and got closer to his wife. He got a lot of support from her. Their relationship was strong, and Ben used his wife as an attentive ear to vent his anger. After a while, this put a lot of tension into the marital relationship. His wife felt she understands his manager, and that Ben, her husband should take responsibility for the way he behaves at work. This raised tension between them, and his wife could no longer contain the situation and moved away on the grounds that she had an important project at work and has to devote herself to it and to her manager. This project was on the table for a year and Jane refused to take it. Now she felt she needed it as a way to distance herself from her needy husband. Ben, instead of taking care of the two tension relationships, with his manager and with his wife, found another detour and dragged a colleague from his work to his work–family triangle. The colleague was happy to use Ben as a detour to his own triangle with the manager.

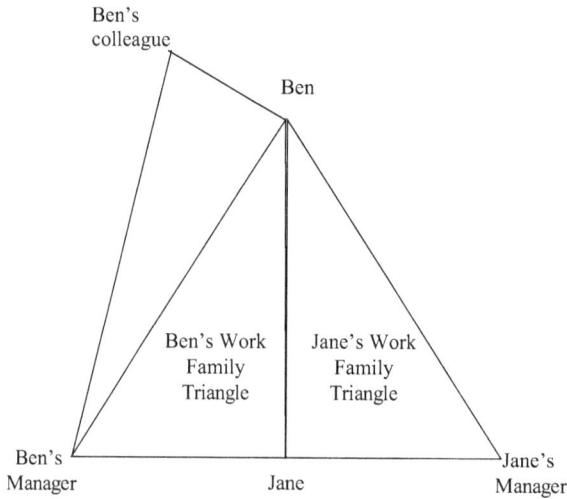

Figure 4.12: Jane and Ben's work–family triangles system.

It is important to understand that the movements did not address the tension – neither between the manager and Ben nor between the couple – they only allowed the tension to be reduced through distancing and creating a detour.

Summarizing this chapter, we used Bowen's triangling process to examine the dynamics of the work–family triangle system and triad relationships. We found that some of the triangling was driven by dyad tension. This tension was found in the three dyads: the work dyad, couple dyad, and manager–spouse dyad. We explored the different possible triangling scenarios. According to Bowen, triangling occurs when the inevitable anxiety in a dyad is relieved by involving a vulnerable third party who either takes sides or provides a detour for the anxiety. An increase in the level of emotional arousal of the individual drives a triangle movement.

One way to understand the movement dynamics is Fogarty's notion of a rubber band holding three people together, where the side length presents the level of involvement, communication, and concern of the dyad players. The rubber band creates a structure that holds the three people in relationship to one another. It forces each to compensate for the movement of either or both other players to keep the band taut.

We found that some triangling was driven by a desirable dyad, which one of the players was interested in strengthening. The triangling dynamic that holds the three people in the triangle space was the same. Whether the triangling was due to tension in a dyad or a desirable dyad, we want the players to synchronize their triangle and not get into a reactive triangle. Chapter 5 elaborates on this process of work–family triangle synchronization (WFTS).

New Concepts in the Chapter

- *Triangling* – Triangling occurs when the inevitable anxiety in a dyad is relieved by involving a vulnerable third party who either takes sides or provides a detour for the anxiety.
- *Work–family triangling (WFT)* – The dynamic that holds the manager, employee, and spouse in a triangle space by compensating for the movement of either or both other players to keep the triangle stable.
- *Work–family triangles system* – The woman's work–family triangle and the man's work–family triangle.
- *Triangle maze* – When the tension in a triangle is too high for the triangle to contain, it spreads to a series of triangles, adding another stakeholder.

WFTS Exercise

Triangle of Life

Practice for all Stakeholders: Managers, Employees and Spouses

Analyze your work–family triangle dynamics using the following questions:

1. Examine the quality of each dyad. Write down the **emotional involvement** of the dyad. Emotional involvement means the level of commitment, engagement, concern, communication, and investment of the dyad. Based on your answer, write the side length in relation to the others, from 1 to 5:
   - Ranking 1 means **a close symbiotic relationship** in which both players are fully committed to and engaged in investing all of their time and effort in the relationship and nothing else.
   - Ranking 2 means **a close and caring relationship**. The players are engaged in this relationship. It is important for them to make sure the relationship is healthy and beneficent for them. They invest time and effort in the relationship. This relationship is very important to them as part of their complete life system.
   - Ranking 3 means that this relationship is **one of their important relationships in life but not one of the main ones**. It is important for the players that it is good and benevolent, and they invest a reasonable amount of thought and time into it.
   - Ranking 4 means a **polite relationship**. The relationship is important to them, but they will not invest in it. It's one of many relationships in their lives, but not one of the most important. It is important that it be respectful and not offensive; however, there is no need to invest and give it significant attention.
   - Ranking 5 means **distance and indifference to the quality of the relationship**. Players do not care about having a good relationship and are not interested in investing in it and in the other player.

Dyad	Detail in your words the emotional involvement of the dyad	Rank the side length (1 to 5)
Work dyad (manager–employee)		
Couple dyad (employee–spouse)		
Employee–spouse dyad		

Draw the triangle according to your ranking:

2. Examine the movement of the triangle. What happens to the triangle when there is tension in one of the relationships? How does the dyad deal with this tension? How does it use the third player to ease the tension?

_____

_____

_____

_____

_____

_____

3. Did the triangular space you drew create fixed roles for some of the players?

_____

_____

_____

_____

4. Draw the other triangles that are part of a work–family triangle maze beyond the work–family triangle:

5. What is the flexibility of the triangle movement? Is there legitimacy for getting closer and further away? Is there reciprocity in the movement? Do you feel it helps manage the work–family interface?

_____

_____

_____

_____

6. Compare your answers with the answers of the other players in the triangle and use this exercise to learn together about the way you manage the work–family space.

_____

_____

_____

_____

References

Bowen, M. (1966). The use of family theory in clinical practice. *Comprehensive Psychiatry*, 7(5), 345–374.

Bowen, M. (1976). Theory in the practice of psychotherapy. *Family Therapy: Theory and Practice*, 4(1), 2–90.

Bowen, M. (1985). *Family therapy in clinical practice*. Jason Aronson.

Brown, J. (1999). Bowen family systems theory and practice: Illustration and critique. *Australian and New Zealand Journal of Family Therapy*, 20(2), 94–103.

Fogarty, T. (1975). Triangles. *The Family*, 2(2), 11–19.

Fogarty, T. (1976). System concepts and the dimensions of self. In P. J. Guerin (Ed.), *Family therapy: Theory and practice* (pp. 144–153). American Psychological Association.

Guerin, P. J., Forarty, T. F., Fay, L. F., & Kautto, J. G. (1996). *Working with relationship triangles: The one-two-three of psychotherapy*. Guilford Press.

Haley, J. (1987). *Problem-solving therapy*. Jossey-Bass.

James, K. (1989). When twos are really threes: The triangular dance in couple conflict. *Australian and New Zealand Journal of Family Therapy, 10*(3), 179–186.

Kerr, M. E., & Bowen, M. (1988). *Family evaluation: The role of the family as an emotional unit that governs individual behavior and development*. Penguin Books.

Minuchin, S. (1974). *Families and family therapy*. Harvard University Press.

Chapter 5
Work–Family Triangle Synchronization (WFTS)

Coming together is a beginning, staying together is progress, and working together is success.
– Henry Ford

In accordance with Henry Ford's quote, it is not enough to understand there are three stakeholders involved in the work–family interface, nor is understanding the dynamics that keep them together; we need them to make a joint effort. Uncovering the dynamic that holds the three stakeholders in the triangle space enables us to find a proactive way to manage the dynamic. We want the stakeholders to synchronize their triangle movement instead of getting into a reactive triangle movement. We name this process *work–family triangle synchronization (WFTS)* .

As noted, many economic and societal changes have affected the work–family interface. Changes include the advancement of communication technologies creating a 24/7 work environment, the employment psychological contract changing from stable long-term settings to short-term unstable settings (from career to employability), increased participation of women in the labor force, and social changes toward gender equality and home roles. These changes affected people differently, depending on their type of work, family status, culture, and unique personality. By synchronizing, we mean that the stakeholders decide together based on their unique context how to manage the complex fit between work and family needs in this new situation.

Work–Family Fit

To explore this fit, we were inspired by person–environment (P–E) fit (the congruence, match, or similarity between the person and the environment) theoretical framework (Caplan, 1987). P–E fit is a widely used theoretical framework in the organizational sciences literature for understanding thinking and behavior. The central hypothesis of the P–E fit theory is that poor fit between the person and environment leads to psychological, physiological, and behavioral strains, which ultimately increase morbidity and mortality. Organizations and their members have a fundamental stake in the goodness of the fit of the characteristics of the person and the environment of the organization. A meta-analysis investigating different types of P–E fit revealed fit to be highly complex, multidimensional constrict with many conceptual definitions (Kristof-Brown et al., 2005). The WFTS model posits that one fit that the organization and individual want to successfully manage is a fit in the work–family interface.

P–E fit can take one of two forms. It can either represent the extent to which the rewards and supplies provided by the environment match the needs and preferences of the person, or it can represent the extent to which the demands and requirements

https://doi.org/10.1515/9783110759808-005

of the environment match the skills and abilities of the person (Edwards & Van Harrison, 1993; Yu, 2009).

Because the work–family interface features two environments (work and family) and three people (manager, employee, and spouse), adapting a person to the environment requires a more complex scheme. Adding the two forms of P–E fit, we argue that in work–family P–E fit, the person is both an individual and an envoy and representative of an environment. The manager is a person with needs and preferences as both an individual and a manager. The manager is also the work representative and as such, represent the work environment's demands and requirements. All those personal needs and preferences and environmental demands and requirements blend. The case of Tomas and Jonathan demonstrates this blend.

> Tomas is a young manager with three little children. He is available to go through the emails that accumulated during the day at 10 p.m., after putting the kids to bed. He expects his employees to answer emails in the late evening hours so he can arrive the next day when "yesterday's things are closed." In contrast, Jonathan prefers to stay in the office until he finishes the day's affairs and gets home when everything is closed. He expects his employees to stay at the office until they finish all the tasks of that day. The work demand they transformed to their employees is a result of the way they chose to comply with the unbiased work demand for addressing emails.

At the same time, the manager has skills and abilities as a person and a manager and has rewards and supplies as the work representative. Again, these skills, abilities, rewards, and supplies blend.

> Thomas believes the workplace needs to be flexible for the sake of the employee. In addition, he has good relationships with HR. As a parent of young children, he understands the constraints of school vacations. He makes sure to get his employees a work-from-home permit so they can be with their children while they are on school vacation and still be connected to work and address work needs. Jonathan, on the other hand, needs control and requires the employees to come to the office so that he can see that they are working and can monitor their work better. Jonathan does not approve working from home for his employees and explains to them that HR only allows this in exceptional cases, and this is not an exceptional case. The work-from-home options differed for Thomas's and Jonathan's employees.

As we see the rewards and supplies provided by the environment (working from home in this example) depend on the representative person's skills, abilities, needs, and preferences. Moreover, the demands and requirements of the environment (availability to address mails) are how the representative person addresses the environment's unbiased needs (addressing mails) based on their skills, abilities, needs, and preferences.

The same goes for the spouse. The spouse has needs and preferences as both an individual and a parent and spouse. The spouse is also the family representative and as such, represent the family environment's demands and requirements. All those spousal needs and preferences and family environment demands and requirements blend. The same goes regarding the spouse's skills, abilities, rewards, and supplies as a person and family representative. The spouse blends as a person and family representative. It is important to note that the family environment includes the couple as part of the family. The spouse as a family representative is a couple representative, too.

The position of the employee in the work–family P–E fit is more complicated. They are part of two environments: work and family. In the employee's case, the demands, requirements, needs, and preferences also blend, reflecting the employee as an individual, parent, spouse, and employee. The same goes regarding the environments' rewards, supplies, demands, and requirements. They blend because the employee is both a work representative and family representative. As discussed later in the chapter, we want all three players to see themselves, to some extent, as representative of the two environments. Otherwise, employees can find themselves "between a rock and a hard place."

Due to these blending factors, we converted P–E fit to P&E–P&E fit, shaping the two forms of P–E fit into two P&E–P&E fit forms: (a) work (as a blend of the work environment, manager, and employee) needs with family (as a blend of family environment, employee, and spouse) knowledge, skills, and abilities (KSA); and (b) family needs (as a blend of family, employee, and spouse) with work (as a blend of work environment, manager, and employee) KSA. Figure 5.1 depicts the manifestation of these two forms in the work–family triangle fit. The work needs–family KSA fit indicates whether the family has the KSA to fit the work needs. For example, can the family cope with a long parental absence due to the work-related travels of the employee? The family needs–work KSA fit refers to the ability of the work KSA to meet family needs. For example, does the work provide the employee with the option to work from home when their child is sick?

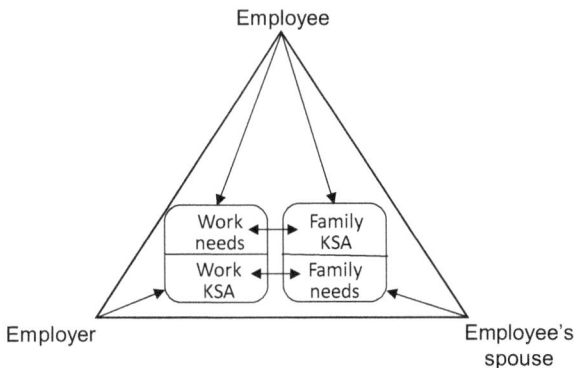

Figure 5.1: Work–family triangle fit.

It is important to recognize that this view, in which work also assesses whether it can meet the needs of the family, is not agreed upon by all stakeholders. Some managers, employees, and spouses we interviewed talked differently about work–family fit. Some indicated that the manager presents the work demands and the employee must find a way to meet them. They do not view the work and family systems as equal such that the two systems should align with each other. Yet today, when workplaces understand the wholeness of the employee (Laloux, 2014) and seek to court employees and retain talent (Bonneton et al., 2019; Harsch & Festing, 2020), the perception has changed; workplaces understand that they must examine their capabilities to meet the needs of the employee's family. This change has only just begun, and a lot of work is required to bring it to the place where it should be according to the WFTS vision, where the three stakeholders make a joint effort to synchronize work and family needs with clever use of work and family KSA.

In dual-earner families, the work–family fit has to handle three environments (man's work environment, woman's work environment, and family environment) and four people (man's manager, woman's manager, man, and woman). Figure 5.2 demonstrates this fit.

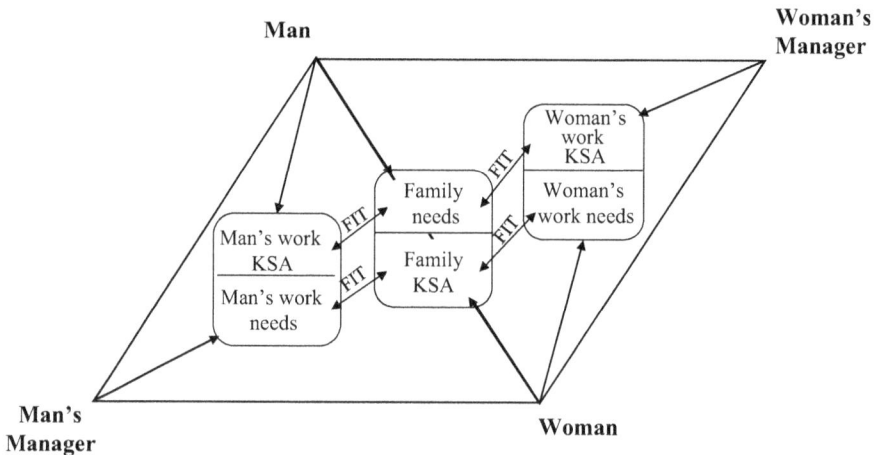

Figure 5.2: Dual-earner work–family triangle fit.

Work–Family Triangle Power Relationship

Managing and attaining work–family triangle fit is a process of exchange relationships. Most exchange relationships in society are characterized by an unequal power distribution between the parties (Aiello et al., 2018; Dwyer & Walker, 1981). Power is a concept that has been investigated exhaustively by scientists and philosophers. Power is also a subject of study in managerial research. Power is not a property of an actor or group, but rather a construct that can be analyzed systematically from the viewpoint of the relationships around an actor. Emerson's (1962) definition is a common operationalization of this construct:

Power resides implicitly in the other's dependency. . . . The dependence of actor A upon actor B is (1) directly proportional to A's motivational investment in goals mediated by B, and (2) can be potentially overcome by A inversely proportional to the availability of those goals to A outside of the A-B relation. . . . The power of actor A over actor B is the amount of resistance on the part of B which can be potentially overcome by A. (p. 32)

In the work and family triangles system, the power relationship is a quartet power relationship – a relationship among the four stakeholders. The four actors (man, woman, man's manager, and woman's manager) are mutually dependent, but not to the same extent, regarding satisfying their demands and needs, mediating and being mediated by the other actors' use of their abilities and supplies and understanding that they are limited in achieving it outside the work–family relationship. The power of each actor is the amount of resistance of other actors that they can potentially overcome. For example, the power of the employee over his manager is realized when he influences the manager to overcome his resistance to delaying the man's business trip.

This quartet power relationship sometimes passes through mediators. In the previous example, it can be that the employee's spouse has power over the employee, her husband, who has power over his manager to overcome his resistance to delaying the man's business trip. An example of two mediators is when the woman's manager influences the man's manager to overcome his resistance to delaying the man's business trip. In this case, the woman's manager has power over the woman, who has power over the man, who has power over his manager. Figure 5.3 depicts this example. The woman's manager's demand for the full availability of the woman for a deadline project (A) results in her requesting that her employee, the woman, use her ability to influence her husband to delay his trip (B). The woman overcomes her husband resistance to confront his manager. To fulfill the man's need to support his wife's career (C), he uses his manager's supply to delay the trip until the next month (D).

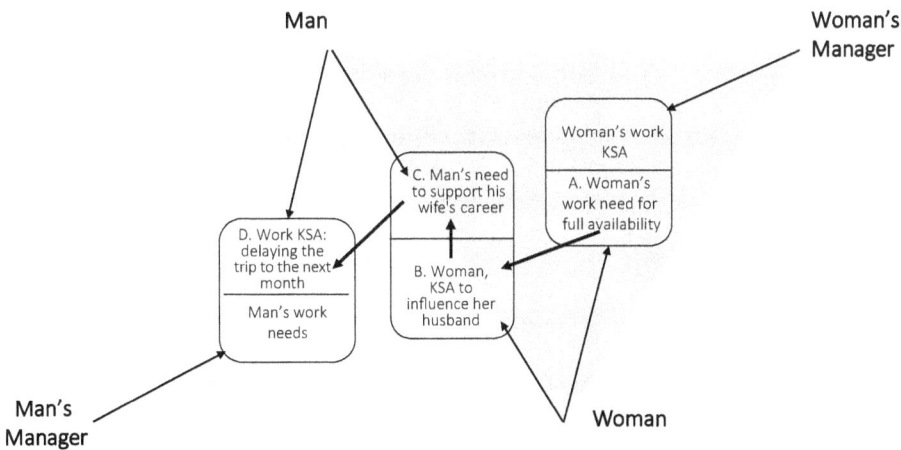

Figure 5.3: Example of work–family triangle power relationship.

In another example, Jane, Bill's manager, wants him to move to manage a division in another country (man's work demand). The couple's ability to relocate now that the children are young (family ability) makes the transition possible only after their need that Robbin, the woman, can work from home (family need) is addressed by her work (woman's work supply). The woman's work requires the move to be for only a year (woman's work demand). The man's work complies (man's work supply). Figure 5.4 depicts this example.

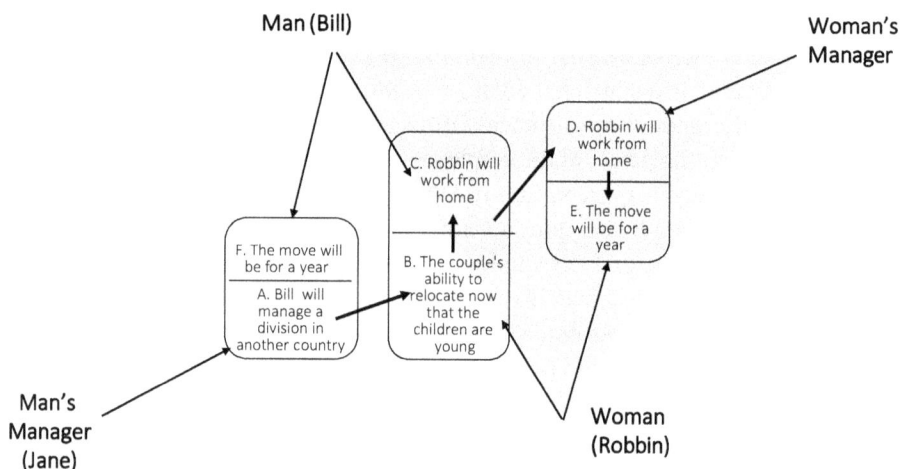

Figure 5.4: Example of work–family triangle power relationship.

Competition vs. Co-Opetition Triangle Power Relationship

We found two types of triangle power relationships controlling the process of work–family fit adjustment: competition and co-opetition. Theoretically, there should be cooperation triangles, too. Unfortunately, we didn't find them. A cooperation work–family triangle means that there is no conflict between work and family needs. All needs can be attained with no need for adjustment. Nowadays, due to economic and social changes, there is an inevitable, predefined, built-in conflict between work and family.

In competition triangles, power was used in a "tug-of-war" way. When the tug-of-war was between the manager and employee or between the members of a couple, the exhibited power relationship was direct. When the tug-of-war was between the manager and the employee's spouse, it was indirect.

In the direct tug-of-war power relationship, the third player can be passive or active. If they are active, a coalition will be created. For example, in one case, the couple pulled together as a coalition in the tug-of-war against a manager who demanded high-level availability. We see the indirect tug-of-war power relationship as "between a rock and a hard place." In this power relationship, the employee manages the tug-of-war between the manager and the spouse, as a messenger. In these cases, we hear conversations such as: "Tell your boss that. . ." or "My wife will kill me if I miss another kindergarten show." The employee does not take a stand and says what he thinks is right, such as saying to the manager that he wants to attend his child's show or saying to his wife that he does not want to attend. As we see it, in these cases, the employee hides behind the spouse or manager and avoids the confrontation, sometimes for good reasons, understanding that confrontation will not be effective because the triangle is not a co-opetition triangle. Figure 5.5 depicts the competition work–family triangle power relationship.

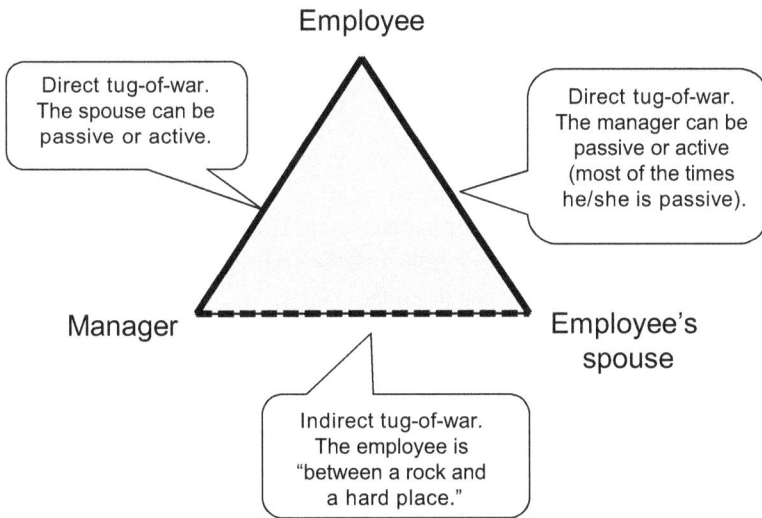

Employee

Direct tug-of-war. The spouse can be passive or active.

Direct tug-of-war. The manager can be passive or active (most of the times he/she is passive).

Manager   Employee's spouse

Indirect tug-of-war. The employee is "between a rock and a hard place."

Figure 5.5: Competition work–family triangle power relationship.

In the case of a *work–family co-opetition power relationship*, each stakeholder takes into consideration the needs and demands of all stakeholders and attempts to find the best work–family fit. The term "co-opetition" is a portmanteau of cooperation and competition. We borrow the term from the business literature, in which it refers to competitors working together to open new markets (Brandenburger & Nalebuff, 1996). The work–family co-opetition power relationship acknowledges the built-in conflict between the spheres and the advantage, for both spheres, to manage this conflict through the cooperation of all stakeholders. A work–family co-opetition power relationship can synchronize work needs–family KSA fit and family needs–work KSA fit, creating *WFTS*. Co-opetition power relationships were found to be effective for empowering triangle fit and reducing triangle tension.

Researching the work–family interface power relationship raises the question of gender equality. Benjamin (2003) expanded the discussion of power from the issues discussed in the marital conversation to the silence theme. Benjamin examined the marital conversations among heterosexual couples and argued that because silencing is an aspect of power relations, the transition from silence to speech is necessarily a process of empowerment. This transition, which she called "unsilencing," is a process in which social relations previously managed in a framework of hegemonic power with what appears to be harmony and agreement ("silencing") become a conflict requiring renewed marital negotiations about arrangements, which in some cases creates a new arrangement. The WFTS process, using the work–family co-opetition power relationship, is a critical part of the unsilencing process, creating a new arrangement – a WFTS psychological contract, a new arrangement that is the optimal fit for all stakeholders.

Work–Family Triangle Synchronization

The stakeholders were familiar with the work–family balance illustration, in which work and family are on a swing and the goal is to strike a balance between them. Some struggled to achieve this, and some stopped trying. The feeling was that this is the theme that society seeks for the work–family interface, a theme that stressed them and many times did not fit their needs and abilities.

WFTS outlines the goal of the work–family interface differently. It does not view an equal level of engagement in the two roles as the goal. We argue that nowadays there is no right or wrong answer regarding the work–family interface, or a "global solution for the work and family problem" as described by some stakeholders. There is a unique answer that fits each system's needs and abilities, a synchronization between the work–family stakeholders regarding the correct way for them to manage the work–family interface.

This goal is closer to work–family balance, aiming to minimize conflict between work and nonwork roles (Clark, 2000), but not the same. WFTS acknowledges that the work and family are in conflict and seeks to manage that work–family conflict in a co-operation power relationship, ensuring the stakeholders to be satisfied with their work–family interface solution.

Our research shows that there is a need to build a process that enables the stakeholders to clarify, negotiate, and shape their own unique solution, their own unique *WFTS psychological contract*. By synchronizing the needs and abilities of the work and family and how they want to handle them, the stakeholders can manage the conflict, improve the way they accomplish their work and family roles, and achieve well-being. This is the WFTS vision.

This vision of a unique, tailored work–family synchronized solution is contrary to family-friendly programs. We argue that there is no solution that suits all work–family triangle systems, no work–family interface that suits all. Studies have shown a gap between the availability and use of family-friendly work practices (McDonald et al.,

2005; Moore, 2018). The WFTS vision can be seen as a step toward the mass customization vision, first coined by Davis (1989), that promotes mass customization as providing individually designed production and services to every customer through high process agility, flexibility, and integration (Da Silveira et al., 2001). Kotha (1996), in his paper on the dynamics of implementing mass customization in a firm that pursues both mass production and mass customization, concluded: "In today's competitive landscape, the issue is not whether the 'mass market' is dead, but finding unique ways of fulfilling changing customer demands" (p. 449). The same can be said now regarding the work–family interface. No mass production suits all work–family triangle systems, no work–family interface suits all. Not the "breadwinner" and "homemaker" solution, not the work–family balance solution, and as studies show, not family-friendly work practices.

Johns (2006) defined context as "situational opportunities and constraints that affect the occurrence and meaning of organizational behavior as well as functional relationships variables" (p. 386). The context of every dual-earner work–family system is different, and stakeholders revealed varied ways of handling the economic and social changes. Therefore, any solution has to be context specific. As elaborated in Chapter 3 on the work–family triangle's dyads, there are three segments that reflect this variance. The first, work–family role, is the way the couple decides to divide their family and work roles. Each of them can be career-focused, family-focused, or both. The second segment, work–family hierarchy, defines which sphere makes the rules and to what extent and which sphere needs to adjust to the other. The third segment, work–family mixture, deals with the extent and intensity with which the two spheres interrelate.

We argue that we have to enter an era of "mass trianglization customization." Each work–family triangle system designs its customized solution to economic and societal changes, creating a solution that suits the system's stakeholders. Society has to give each work–family triangle system the freedom and the tools to do so. Freedom means that the solution of the system is not judged. A senior manager sadly told us about the significant criticism she receives from friends and colleagues for the fact that she and her husband decided she would invest in her career, including many flights for extended periods, and he would take a less demanding job that allows him to be home with the kids every day. As for tools, Chapter 6, WFTS psychological contract, offers a practical method for this process.

New Concepts in the Chapter
- *Work–family triangle synchronization (WFTS)* – The process by which the stakeholders synchronize, threw co-opetition, their needs and KSA to generate the triangle fit that suits them.
- *Work–family triangle fit* – The fit between the work and family needs using work and family KSA. This fit is composed of (a) the work needs–family KSA fit, or the family's use of knowledge, skills, and abilities to fit the work needs; and (b) the family needs–work KSA fit, which refers to the knowledge, skills, and abilities of work to meet family needs.

- *Dual-earner family work–family triangle fit* – The fit between the man's work needs, woman's work needs, and family needs using their KSA wisely to achieve the best WFTS.
- *Work–family co-opetition power relationship* – A clever cooperative use of work and family KSA to resolve the in-built conflict brought on by the competition between work and family for time, attention, and significance.
- *WFTS psychological contract* – The unique solution of the triangle stakeholders synchronizing the needs and KSA of work and family.

References

Aiello, A., Tesi, A., Pratto, F., & Pierro, A. (2018). Social dominance and interpersonal power: Asymmetrical relationships within hierarchy-enhancing and hierarchy-attenuating work environments. *Journal of Applied Social Psychology*, *48*(1), 35–45.

Benjamin, O. (2003). The power of unsilencing: Between silence and negotiation in heterosexual relationships. *Journal for the Theory of Social Behaviour*, *33*(1), 1–19.

Bonneton, D., Schworm, S. K., Festing, M., & Muratbekova-Touron, M. (2019). Do global talent management programs help to retain talent? A career-related framework. *The International Journal of Human Resource Management*. Advance online publication. https://doi.org/10.1080/09585192.2019.1683048

Brandenburger, A. M., & Nalebuff, B. J. (1996). *Co-opetition*. Harvard Business School Press.

Caplan, R. D. (1987). Person-environment fit theory and organizations: Commensurate dimensions, time perspectives, and mechanisms. *Journal of Vocational Behavior*, *31*(3), 248–267.

Clark, S. C. (2000). Work/family border theory: A new theory of work/family balance. *Human Relations*, *53*(6), 747–770.

Da Silveira, G., Borenstein, D., & Fogliatto, F. S. (2001). Mass customization: Literature review and research directions. *International Journal of Production Economics*, *72*(1), 1–13.

Davis, S. M. (1989). From "future perfect": Mass customizing. *Planning Review*, *17*(2), 16–21.

Dwyer, F. R., & Walker, O. C., Jr. (1981). Bargaining in an asymmetrical power structure. *Journal of Marketing*, *45*(1), 104–115.

Edwards, J. R., & Van Harrison, R. (1993). Job demands and worker health: Three-dimensional reexamination of the relationship between person environment fit and strain. *Journal of Applied Psychology*, *78*(4), 628–648.

Emerson, R. M. (1962). Power-dependence relations. *American Sociological Review*, *27*(1), 31–41.

Greenhaus, J. H., Collins, K. M., & Shaw, J. D. (2003). The relation between work–family balance and quality of life. *Journal of Vocational Behavior*, *63*(3), 510–531.

Harsch, K., & Festing, M. (2020). Dynamic talent management capabilities and organizational agility – A qualitative exploration. *Human Resource Management*, *59*(1), 43–61.

Johns, G. (2006). The essential impact of context on organizational behavior. *Academy of Management Review*, *31*(2), 386–408.

Kirchmeyer, C. (2000). Work-life initiatives: Greed or benevolence regarding workers' time? *Trends in Organizational Behavior*, *7*, 79–94.

Kotha, S. (1996). From mass production to mass customization: The case of the National Industrial Bicycle Company of Japan. *European Management Journal*, *14*(5), 442–450.

Kristof-Brown, A. L., Zimmerman, R. D., & Johnson, E. C. (2005). Consequences of individuals' fit at work: A meta-analysis of person–job, person–organization, person–group, and person–supervisor fit. *Personnel Psychology*, *58*(2), 281–342.

Laloux, F. (2014). *Reinventing organizations: A guide to creating organizations inspired by the next stage in human consciousness.* Nelson Parker.

McDonald, P., Brown, K., & Bradley, L. (2005). Explanations for the provision-utilisation gap in work-life policy. *Women in Management Review, 20*(1), 37–55.

Moore, T. S. (2018). Why don't employees use family-friendly work practices? *Asia Pacific Journal of Human Resources, 58*(1), 3–23.

Sirgy, M. J., & Lee, D.-J. (2018). Work-life balance: An integrative review. *Applied Research in Quality of Life, 13*(1), 229–254.

Yu, K. Y. T. (2009). Affective influences in person–environment fit theory: Exploring the role of affect as both cause and outcome of PE fit. *Journal of Applied Psychology, 94*(5), 1210–1226.

Chapter 6
WFTS Psychological Contract

> A contract is only as good as the people signing it.
> – Jeffrey Fry

After discussing the WFTS vision for a unique, tailored work–family synchronized solution, we want to propose a tool for designing the solution: the *"WFTS triaxial contract."* As Jeffery Fry stated, the main aspect in designing the contract is the people's cooperation and good intentions. In a work–family co-opetition power relationship (discussed in Chapter 5), each stakeholder considers the needs of all stakeholders and attempts to find the optimal work–family fit. The sincere intention of the players is the crucial aspect. The WFTS triaxial contract is a tool that invites them to bring their intentions to fruition.

To design this contract, the stakeholders have to map the needs of the family, give them recognition and legitimization, and then explore the knowledge, skills, and abilities (KSA) of the two workplaces (the man's work and the woman's work) that can enable the fulfilment of the needs. At the same time, they have to map the two workplaces' needs and the various family KSA that can allow these needs to be fulfilled. Recognition of the works and family needs and discussions about how to engage them, using their KSA, is an active way to manage the work–family interface. Achieving a WFTS psychological contract involves acknowledging conflict and ensuring interest in finding a way that will use the work and family KSA to manage the conflict in the best way toward the well-being of all stakeholders.

Unfortunately, in many cases, stakeholders do not sincerely try to understand the needs to find the best way to meet them. Instead, they perceive the work and family interface as a competition where every side tries to meet maximum needs with minimum use of their KSA – a "minimum investment, maximum achievement" perception. To win this competition, stakeholders underestimate the importance of the needs of the other and overestimate their needs. The WFTS triaxial contract invites all stakeholders to change this unproductive strategy and acknowledge all needs. Acknowledging them does not necessarily mean fulfilling them. It means recognizing the needs of each player and understanding that in cooperation, others can cooperate and find an appropriate solution for the work and family competition and that all have to engage in this challenge together. There are no winners and losers, only all winners or all losers. It is better to recognize the needs and explain what can be done than to deny them. Denying leaves stakeholders with the feeling that they are alone and have to fight for their legitimate needs.

To make sure that the needs mapping is holistic and thorough, we use Dolan's triaxial model (Dolan, 2011).

https://doi.org/10.1515/9783110759808-006

Dolan's Triaxial Model

The triaxial model (Dolan, 2011) argues that a balanced set of values that will lead to well-being has to include three axes of values: the economic–pragmatic axis, the ethical–social axis, and the emotional–developmental axis.

The economic–pragmatic axis includes values relating to efficiency, performance standards, and discipline. These values guide such activities as planning, professionalism, and organizing. The ethical–social axial deals with how people behave in a group. Ethical–social values emerge from beliefs held about how people should conduct themselves in public, at work, and in relationships. They are associated with such values as honesty, congruence, respect, and loyalty, to name a few. The third axis is the emotional–developmental axis. This axis relates to intrinsic motivation, to what makes us excited and believe in a cause. Optimism, passion, energy, freedom, and happiness are a few examples of such values.

Analyzing work and family needs revealed in interviews and consultations, we found that using Dolan's three conceptual axes provides a rich, holistic, thorough, and detailed way of mapping work and family needs. We divided work and family needs into the three axes according to the motive of each need. We named the first axis "*work–family functional–pragmatic needs*." These needs have a functional–pragmatic motive, such as a family need that the employee takes the children to school in the morning because the spouse has to leave the house early or a family need that the employee will work from home when the child is sick. An example of a work functional–pragmatic need is the need to answer client calls on weekends or fly on a day's notice to visit a client.

We named the second axis "*work–family relational needs*." The motive in this case is a good relationship in the dyad. Needs might include a spouse's request of her husband that "when we eat, no work phone calls, please" or a manager's request of her employee:

> I need our relationship [manager–employee dyad] to be more reciprocal. Whenever you [the employee] needed help, I came to your aid, but when I needed you to be flexible and to take into consideration my needs so the work will be done, I saw no understanding.

The third axis is named "*work–family personal–emotional needs*," which are needs driven by a personal–emotional motive; frequently, they involve the need to be seen. An example of such a need is an employee expecting sensitivity and consideration in light of his child being hospitalized. When the employee told his manager that he would be late the next day because he would be in the hospital at night, the manager answered: "It is problematic but OK," without any sensitivity or asking about the child's condition. A family need can come from the spouse to the employee, like the spouse stating: "I do not want to schedule things through your secretary. I am your wife, and I want to talk and schedule with you." This was revealed after a big fight with her husband when she wanted to go with him to lunch and he asked her to check with his secretary about when it would be most convenient. An example of a work personal–emotional need is a case in which a manager requested that an employee not to abuse her understanding of family needs. This occurred after she complied many times with the employee's request to leave early because of family needs. She felt he did not respect and recognize her consideration and underestimated her efforts.

Because the work–family triangle consists of two spheres (work and family), three dyads (manager–employee, employee–spouse, and manager–spouse), and three stakeholders (manager, employee, and spouse), needs can be raised by any stakeholder as a need of a sphere as they understand it, the need of a dyad, or a personal need. A need can be perceived by one of the stakeholders as a need of the sphere, whereas another stakeholder might think otherwise. For example, a manager can raise a work need "to arrive at work on time in the morning," whereas the employee might think it is not necessary and view the need as a control need of the manager and not a business need. It does not matter which is right – when mapping needs, all stakeholders raise their needs according to their understanding. In the second stage, when addressing needs, a discussion is held to understand the extent to which a need is critical and solvable.

Tables 6.1 and 6.2 display examples of work–family triaxial needs. Table 6.1 details family needs organized by axis. Table 6.2 details work needs organized by axis. Further examples can be found in the Appendix.

Table 6.1: Work–family triaxial: Family needs.

Axis	Family needs raised by employee or spouse
Functional–pragmatic needs	To be at home, present, and available by 17:00
Functional–pragmatic needs	To be available to family members' calls when working
Relational needs	A day once a week when we (as a couple or family) spend time together
Relational needs	To be available to be with the kids and me when you return from work without interruption from work
Personal–emotional needs	To respect my work [every time one of the parents had to stay home with a child, his wife explained to him that his work is more flexible and he should stay home because she can't miss a day]
Personal–emotional needs	To call me when you are at work, take an interest in my day, and ask if I need anything

Table 6.2: Work–family triaxial: Work needs.

Axis	Work needs raised by manager or employee
Functional–pragmatic needs	To be concentrated and focused on the job, even when there are problems at home
Functional–pragmatic needs	To be responsive to work matters after working hours
Relational needs	To bring your spouse to work events [the manager saw it as an act of commitment]
Relational needs	Reciprocal consideration [a manager felt that she is very considerate, but when she asks her employee for consideration, she refused]
Personal–emotional needs	Not to abuse my understanding of family needs
Personal–emotional needs	Not to burden my work with all the family needs; that your spouse will help, too

As seen from the table, some needs can be seen as functional, but discussion revealed the underlying relational or personal need. A need like "react to my messages throughout the day" can be understood as functional, requesting a reaction to manage things that pop up during the day. But a deeper exploration revealed that when he answered pragmatically, the need was not filled. It made things even worse. That is why it is important to understand the motive of the need before trying to fulfill it.

Attributing a need to one of the axes gives it meaning. When stakeholders see the same request through a different axial lens, they do not understand the reaction of the other. In the example where the spouse did not want to schedule plans with her husband through his secretary, the employee saw it as a pragmatic request ("She knows my schedule constraints better than I do") and the spouse saw it as a rude, insulting request that did not recognize her personal–emotional need to be seen as his wife rather than an appointment to squeeze into his schedule.

After mapping their needs and before exploring the KSA that can address these needs, the stakeholders should synchronize the three psychological contract segments noted in Chapter 3: (a) work–family hierarchy, (b) work–family mixture, and (c) work–family role. We use the mapped needs to understand the segments. The need is the output of how we address conflict through the work–family perception lens. For example, a family need of "be home by 19:00 for a family supper without phone calls three times a week" features an underlying perception that the work and family roles are complementary. The man is career focused (segment: work–family roles). The work and family compromise and adjust to the meet the other sphere's needs (segment: work–family hierarchy). And the work and family are separated, meaning when the employee is at work, their attention is at work, and when they are at home, their full attention is at home with the family (segment: work–family mixture). Understanding the segments that created the need enables the stakeholders to synchronize the work–family interface perception, a perception that the KSA will address later in the process.

The mapped needs are a manifestation of the full set of needs, both work and family. These needs are the central needs that are currently producing a conflict. Synchronizing the perception of the interface, through synchronizing the segments, will allow stakeholders to not only address the specific needs that have been mapped, but also give their perception of the response to additional needs that will arise in the process. In other words, the WFTS psychological contract is both a concrete response to the aspects that we identified as the core of the conflict and a comprehensive perceptual response to the conflicts that will arise daily.

In sum, the work–family triaxial psychological contract has to address both required fits: (a) the work needs–family KSA fit and (b) the family needs–work KSA fit. Every fit element in the WFTS triaxial contract includes:

(a) The axis of the need: functional–pragmatic, relational, or personal–emotional
(b) The need
(c) The need's work–family segments: work–family hierarchy, work–family mixture, or work–family role. The need is based on a specific assumption as to the correct way to address the work–family segments.
(d) The KSA that can address the need
(e) The synchronized perception of the work–family segments as a result of the fit synchronization

Tables 6.3 and 6.4 detail two examples of fit elements; Table 6.3 features a fit element of a family need, and Table 6.4 features a fit element of a work need. The Appendix contains more examples of family needs–work KSA fit and work needs–family KSA fit.

Table 6.3: WFTS triaxial contract: Family need–work KSA fit element.

Axis	Relational need
Family need	Be home by 19:00 for a family supper without phone calls three times a week
Work–family segment perceptions	– Work–family roles: complementary triangles system where the man is career focused – Work–family hierarchy: work and family compromise and adjust to the meet the other sphere's needs – Work–family mixture: work–family separation
Work KSA	Unable to commit, but can try to be home at 20:00 and answer work phone calls only after supper
Work–family segment perceptions after fit synchronization	– Work–family roles: No change; consistent with the original family perception – Work–family hierarchy: No change; consistent with the original family perception – Work–family mixture: Updated work–family interaction

Table 6.4: WFTS triaxial contract: Work need–family KSA fit element.

Axis	Functional–pragmatic needs
Work need	To be at work at 08:00
Work–family segment perceptions	– Work–family roles: Irrelevant – Work–family hierarchy: Family or spouse compromises and adjusts to the work needs – Work–family mixture: Irrelevant
Family KSA	Cannot do it, have to take the children to school
Work–family segment perceptions after fit synchronization	– Work–family roles: Career and family focused – Work–family hierarchy: Work and family compromise and adjust to meet the other sphere's needs – Work–family mixture: Irrelevant

WFTS Triaxial Contract Design Process

The process of designing the WFTS triaxial contract is a continual process of many synchronization discussions in different stakeholder settings. Some synchronization discussions involve the couple, some involve the employee and the manager, some are triangle discussions, and in some cases, some occur between the manager and the spouse. It takes several iterations to make sure everyone is synchronized, thinks they can make the necessary modifications and adjustments, and feels that their needs have been addressed, even if not entirely fulfilled. We refer to these synchronization discussions as "sync talks."

In most cases, the process is composed of iterations of couple sync talks and manager–employee sync talks (man's manager–employee and woman's manager–employee sync talks). The couple is the intermediary between the two managers. In other cases in which the manager and spouse know each other and the three stakeholders feel comfortable with one another, they can have a triangle sync talk. In some cases, we found that manager–spouse sync talks enable a focused and effective process that promotes the contract. In those cases, the employee feels comfortable about the manager and spouse openly communicating and appropriately managing the synchronization.

It is recommended that before a sync talk, every stakeholder individually identify the work and family needs as they understand them. Then the stakeholders should reflect on the current work–family psychological contract. They should have an open dialogue regarding how the work–family interface currently operates. At this point, it is important not to assess whether they are satisfied with the psychological contract, but to find out how they think things are going. Only then should they discuss the identified needs to understand what each one means and its significance. As noted, the mapped needs are a manifestation of the full set of central needs currently producing the conflict. Stakeholders should reflect on the three psychological contract segments and use the mapped needs to discuss and synchronize the segments. When the segments are synchronized, the stakeholders can openly discuss and find a proper way to meet those needs, taking into account the work and family KSA.

Some triangles can carry out this process alone, whereas others will prefer to involve a professional who can help reveal the situation and shape the contract they want. Each dyad and triangle has to decide whether they are interested in carrying out the process independently or with the guidance of a professional.

Work–Family Triangle Satisfaction

Borrowing from the Satisfaction with Life Scale (Diener et al., 1985), we defined the satisfaction of each stakeholder with the WFTS triaxial contract as the extent to which they perceive the contract is close to their ideal contract, the conditions of contract are excellent, the contract includes the important things they want in the work–family interface, and the extent to which they would not change the contract.

Analyzing many contracts, we concluded that satisfaction with the WFTS triaxial contract can be described on a continuum, as depicted in Figure 6.1, containing the following stages:
1. Ideal: The fit contract is good for me.
2. Adjustment: I made personal adjustments so that the fit contract would suit me.
3. Compromise: I can live with the fit contract without feeling dissatisfied or exploited.
4. Frustration: I feel that I chose without a real alternative. I feel I cannot choose my preferred contract because when my partner's needs are not met, the cost is too severe and not worth it.
5. Helpless: I am not satisfied with the existing fit contract, but I cannot change it no matter how hard I try.

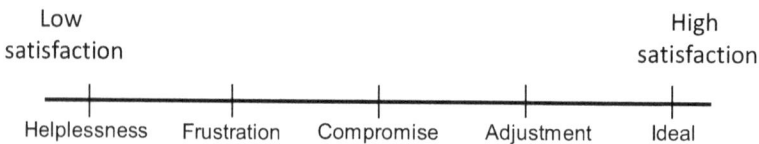

Figure 6.1: Work–family triangle satisfaction.

Satisfaction with the contract is not static. In one triangle, the man was synchronized with his wife regarding the understanding that he will be devoted to work and she will be focused on raising the children. After 10 years, he changed his perception and wanted his wife to start working for economic reasons and because he felt she was boring and neglecting herself. His satisfaction changed from ideal to helpless. She was happy with her lifestyle. The children grew up, and she finally had time to herself. She had no professional skills and did not want to start learning.

Another example is a triangle in which the woman loved being married to a successful businessman, but as the years went by, she felt alone with no partner and wanted him to spend more time at home. He was developing his career and had no interest in changing. Her satisfaction changed from ideal to adjustment to compromise. Understanding that this was the situation, she started building a friend circle and interests. Her husband told us that he knows it might end in divorce, but he cannot see himself making a dramatic change in his life. He is at the peak of his career.

Couples that have changed their satisfaction in a positive direction were those that opened and built a new psychological contract that suited them both. Some achieved this in couples therapy and some on their own.

An interesting process occurred in some couples when the spouse felt helpless and to avoid this unpleasant feeling, made a rational move to the position of frustration. Some did this with full awareness and some without. Understanding that this was their life situation, they preferred "choosing" it over being a victim. One of the interviewees said: "I know this is who he is. I cannot change it, and even if I could, I would get a frustrated husband at home, and it would be worse. For some years, I felt helpless and hated the feeling."

Analyzing the satisfaction of the contract in the work environment also revealed cases in which the stakeholders changed their satisfaction with the contract. In one case, the employee was very committed to the job and adapted his family to the job requirements. After his spouse demanded a change of contract, he started adapting his work to the needs of the family. His manager tried to reinstate the original contract but was unsuccessful. From a position in which he was very satisfied with the contract, the ideal stage, the manager moved to frustration very quickly.

These examples highlight the interdependence among the environment, family and work, and the need to synchronize the contract among all stakeholders through coopetition rather than competition. In the following section, we explore how stakeholders respond to dissatisfaction with the contract.

Work–Family Triangle Misfit

Person–environment fit theory concludes that misfits between the person and the environment leads to psychological, physiological, and behavioral strains, which ultimately increase morbidity and mortality (Caplan, 1987; Edwards & Van Harrison, 1993). Work–family triangle misfits have the same results. Analyzing the consequences of work–family triangle misfit is important to understand the significance of the WFTS process.

Hirschman's (1970) exit, voice, loyalty, and neglect framework describes four employee responses to dissatisfaction with psychological contracts: (a) exit behavior, or leaving without trying to fix things; (b) voice behavior, or speaking up and attempting to remedy the defects, taking reasonable initiative in a belief that conditions can be improved, offering open discussions, and providing solutions; (c) loyalty, or decreasing involvement in extra role and organizational citizenship behavior; and (d) neglect behavior, or halfheartedly participating, reducing active involvement, ignoring responsibility, and being late or absent. Farrell (1983) argued that the responses can be separated into two dimensions: constructive (voice, loyalty) or destructive (exit, neglect).

Examining stakeholders' responses to a work–family triangle misfit, we found the same four categories. Stakeholders who were dissatisfied with the contract and believed that there was a point in talking about the fit and changing the contract tried to do so. Some did it independently, and some enlisted the help of professionals. If the response involved the couple, they were assisted by a couples therapist; if it was a manager–employee dyad, they were assisted by a human resources expert or organizational consultant. Attempting to improve compatibility through conversations is similar to the WFTS process, even if done in a different format than suggested here. Sometimes, a conversation between the dyad's members – the couple or the work dyad – was enough. Sometimes, after the dyad process, a follow-up conversation with the other dyad was required. After the couple's fit conversation, a conversation with the manager was required, and after a manager–employee fit conversation, a couple conversation was required.

When stakeholders thought that there was no point in talking about a new work family fit, the reaction was of a decrease in loyalty. The stakeholders were less committed to the relationship, whether it was the couple relationship or the work relationship. Dedication and investment in the relationship went down. The feeling was that there was nothing to do but compromising and accepting the fit. Sometimes the players made small attempts to improve the situation, often in unilateral steps. Rope pulling operations as mentioned in the previous chapter.

After a period, when the rope pulling operations did not help and the stakeholder did not see a change in the contract, some began to move to neglect respond. At work this is reflected in neglect of work responsibilities, with some tasks done negligently or not at all. A similar thing happened in the family environment when the frustration stemmed from the couple's part of the contract. One partner began to neglect their parenting and family tasks. They did the minimum without the emotional commitment required.

When unhappiness with the contract increased and neglectful acts failed to allay the intensity of the anger, some stakeholders chose to leave – the exit response. In the work environment, exit means the resignation of the employee. When the employee's neglectful responses led the manager to an understanding that they did not have the ability to change the contract and force the employee to exhibit proper conduct, the exit was reflected in the dismissal of the employee. In the family environment, the exit meant separation. Leaving the family environment is more significant and therefore, more attempts are often made before choosing this response. Sometimes after the neglect response, stakeholders returned to the voice response and made repeated attempts to resolve dissatisfaction with the contract through conversation, independently or with professional help. In some cases in the work environment, the neglect response led to a return to the conversation – the voice response – but these cases were less common than in the family environment.

Reciprocity of Work Needs–Family KSA Fit and Family Needs–Work KSA Fit

In our exploration of the dependence between the two forms of work–family fit – work needs–family KSA fit and family needs–work KSA fit – we found that in most cases, there was no expectation of an equivalence between the extent to which work addresses family needs and vice versa. One way to explain it is through *work–family hierarchy*. When asymmetric exists and one sphere (work or family) is above the other, it is reasonable for the stakeholders to believe that the lower sphere will be more considerate than the higher.

It is important to distinguish between expecting equivalence and expecting fairness, caring, and trustworthiness. Equivalence means that the effort the work sphere makes to meet family needs is equal to the effort the family makes to meet work needs. In most cases, there was no expectation of equivalence. Fairness, caring, and trustworthiness mean mutual respect of work and family needs and a commitment to fulfill the work–family triaxial fit psychological contract.

An example that clarifies the difference between equivalence and fairness is the Liam, James, and Taylor case.

> Their WFTS involves work–family role type 4: The man is work focused and the woman is family focused, the work–family hierarchy is that the family compromises and adjusts to work needs, the work–family mixture is work–family interaction, and the work–family triaxial fit psychological contract requires no work calls on weekends. In this system, Taylor, the woman, does not expect an equal work–family balance. She knows and accepts that on workdays, work always has the upper hand. But if Liam, the manager, calls James on a Friday night, this is a violation of the contract. Liam has to respect the contract as she respects it.

The more the contract is unbalanced, the greater the expectation of reliability. We found that when one stakeholder felt that the other stakeholders were trying to meet the stakeholder's needs as synchronized in the contract, they were more willing to sacrifice their needs. Chapter 7, on trust in work–family triangles, elaborates on this reliability expectation.

New Concepts in the Chapter
- *WFTS triaxial contract* – A tool enabling the stakeholders to design a psychological contract that addresses the work and family axes by creating a family needs–work KSA fit and a work needs–family KSA fit for the three axial needs.
- *Work–family functional–pragmatic needs* – Work and family needs driven by functional–pragmatic motives.
- *Work–family relationship needs* – Work and family needs driven by a motive of a good relationship among the dyads.
- *Work–family personal–emotional needs* – Work and family needs driven by a personal–emotional motive.

Appendix: WFTS Triaxial Contract: Examples of Fit Elements

WFTS triaxial contract: Family needs.

Axis	Family needs raised by employee or spouse
Functional–pragmatic needs	Be at home, present, and available by 17:00
Functional–pragmatic needs	Be available to family members' calls when working
Functional–pragmatic needs	Flexibility; help pick up the children from school when needed
Functional–pragmatic needs	Be home until 18:00 on Wednesdays due to my spouse's other commitments
Functional–pragmatic needs	Do not work on weekends and holidays [Can be a relationship need, too, depending on the motivation of the need. A functional need: Be available to play with the kids because my spouse works on weekends or feels it's complicated to be with the kids alone. A relationship need: Be together as a family on the weekend.]
Functional–pragmatic needs	Arrive home on time when we have plans
Relational needs	Spend time together as a couple or family one day a week
Relational needs	Take into consideration the needs of both businesses, not only yours
Relational needs	Be available to be with the kids and me when you return from work without interruption from work
Relational needs	Do not work on the weekends; be with the family
Relational needs	Arrive at events on time (e.g., birthday and preschool parties)
Relational needs	Be home by 19:00 for a family supper three times a week
Relational needs	Call me and ask how I am without a functional reason
Relational needs	Do not answer every work call, only important ones (and not all calls are important)
Relational needs	Once a year, take 3 weeks off work to go on a family vacation abroad
Personal–emotional needs	Respect my work [every time one parent had to stay home with a child, the woman explained to her spouse that his work is more flexible and he should stay because she can't miss a day]
Personal–emotional needs	Be attentive to the problems and crises of the children [the woman felt that she had to handle all the children's matters and she could not even speak to him about them]
Personal–emotional needs	Call me when you are at work, take an interest in my day, and ask if I need anything
Personal–emotional needs	React to my messages throughout the day
Personal–emotional needs	Know when you will get home from work and that you meet the time commitment

WFTS triaxial contract: Work needs.

Axis	Work needs raised by manager or employee
Functional–pragmatic needs	Concentrate and focus on the job, even when there are problems at home
Functional–pragmatic needs	Be responsive to work matters after working hours
Functional–pragmatic needs	Arrive at work on time in the morning
Functional–pragmatic needs	Attend important meetings even when they are late in the day
Functional–pragmatic needs	Be available for emergency flights without advance notice
Relational needs	Bring your spouse to work events [the manager saw it as an act of commitment]
Relational needs	Practice reciprocal consideration [a manager that felt that she is very considerate but when she asks her employee for consideration, she refuses]
Personal–emotional needs	Do not abuse my understanding of family needs
Personal–emotional needs	Do not burden my work with all the family needs; ensure that your spouse helps, too

Family needs–work KSA fit elements.

Example 1	
Axis	Functional–pragmatic need
Family need	**Be available to answer family members' calls when working**
Work–family segment perceptions	– Work–family roles: Career and family focused – Work–family hierarchy: Work and family both compromise and adjust to the meet the other sphere's needs – Work–family mixture: Work–family interaction
Work KSA	**Available when working in an office, but not when in a conference**
Work–family segment perceptions after fit synchronization	As assumed
Example 2	
Axis	Functional–pragmatic needs
Family need	**Do not bring your work home**
Work–family segment perceptions	– Work–family roles: Career and family focused – Work–family hierarchy: Work compromises and adjusts to family needs – Work–family mixture: Work–family separation

Work KSA	**Cannot comply; when home, can work after 20:00 when children are asleep**
Work–family segment perceptions after fit synchronization	– Work–family roles: As assumed – Work–family hierarchy: As assumed – Work–family mixture: Work–family interaction

Example 3

Axis	Functional–pragmatic need
Family need	**Be flexible and help pick up the children from school when needed**
Work–family segment perceptions	– Work–family roles: Career and family focused – Work–family hierarchy: Work and family both compromise and adjust to the meet the other sphere's needs – Work–family mixture: Irrelevant
Work KSA	**Cannot always comply, only in exceptional cases**
Work–family segment perceptions after fit synchronization	– Work–family roles: Complementary triangles system where the man is career focused – Work–family hierarchy: The woman's work compromises and adjusts to family needs – Work–family mixture: Irrelevant

Example 4

Axis	Relational need
Family need	**Do not answer every work call, only important ones (and not all calls are important)**
Work–family segment perceptions	– Work–family roles: Career and family focused – Work–family hierarchy: Work and family both compromise and adjust to meet the other sphere's needs – Work–family mixture: Work–family interaction
Work KSA	**The manager will indicate if a call is urgent; otherwise, answer only if it is convenient**
Work–family segment perceptions after fit synchronization	As assumed

Example 5

Axis	Personal–emotional need
Family need	**React to my messages throughout the day**
Work–family segment perceptions	– Work–family roles: Career and family focused – Work–family hierarchy: Work and family both compromise and adjust to the meet the other sphere's needs – Work–family mixture: Irrelevant

Work KSA	**Cannot answer unless it's urgent**
Work–family segment perceptions after fit synchronization	– Work–family roles: Complementary triangles system where the man is career focused – Work–family hierarchy: The woman (and not only her work) compromises and adjusts to work needs – Work–family mixture: (Close to) work–family separation

Example 6	
Axis	Personal–emotional need
Family need	**Call me when you are at work, take an interest in my day, and ask if I need anything**
Work–family segment perceptions	– Work–family roles: Irrelevant – Work–family hierarchy: Irrelevant – Work–family mixture: Work–family interaction
Work KSA	**I will be happy to do so**
Work–family segment perceptions after fit synchronization	As assumed

Work needs–family KSA fit elements.

Example 1	
Axis	Functional–pragmatic need
Work need	**Fly whenever we need you to see a client**
Work–family segment perceptions	– Work–family roles: Irrelevant – Work–family hierarchy: Family or spouse work compromises and adjusts to work needs – Work–family mixture: Irrelevant
Family KSA	**Cannot; my wife has a demanding career, too. I can fly once a month. We have to prioritize the clients' requests.**
Work–family segment perceptions after fit synchronization	– Work–family roles: Career and family focused – Work–family hierarchy: Work and family compromise and adjust to the meet the other sphere's needs – Work–family mixture: Irrelevant

Example 2	
Axis	Functional–pragmatic need
Work need	**Attend important meetings even when they are late**
Work–family segment perceptions	– Work–family roles: Irrelevant – Work–family hierarchy: Family or spouse work compromises and adjusts to work needs – Work–family mixture: Irrelevant

Family KSA	**Only if we know about the meeting a few days ahead and I can organize it with my husband**
Work–family segment perceptions after fit synchronization	– Work–family roles: Career and family focused – Work–family hierarchy: Work and family compromise and adjust to the meet the other sphere's needs – Work–family mixture: Irrelevant

Example 3

Axis	Relational needs
Work need	**Bring your spouse to work events**
Work–family segment perceptions	– Work–family roles: Irrelevant – Work–family hierarchy: Irrelevant – Work–family mixture: Work–family interaction
Family KSA	**Don't want to and don't understand why it is so important; my wife is not part of my work**
Work–family segment perceptions after fit synchronization	– Work–family roles: Irrelevant – Work–family hierarchy: Irrelevant – Work–family mixture: Work–family separation

Example 4

Axis	Relational need
Work need	**Be reciprocally considerate [a manager felt that she is very considerate but when she asks her employee for consideration, she refuses]**
Work–family segment perceptions	– Work–family roles: Irrelevant – Work–family hierarchy: Work and family both compromise and adjust to the meet the other sphere's needs – Work–family mixture: Irrelevant
Family KSA	**Work has more resources than I do and needs to come toward the employee; my family cannot adjust to work needs**
Work–family segment perceptions after fit synchronization	– Work–family roles: Irrelevant – Work–family hierarchy: Work compromises and adjusts to family needs – Work–family mixture: Irrelevant

Example 5

Axis	Personal–emotional need
Work need	**Do not abuse my understanding of family needs**
Work–family segment perceptions	– Work–family roles: Irrelevant – Work–family hierarchy: Work and family compromise and adjust to the meet the other sphere's needs – Work–family mixture: Irrelevant

Family KSA	**OK, I will ask for work adjustment only when I really need your understanding. In those cases, please address my needs.**
Work–family segment perceptions after fit synchronization	As assumed

Example 6	
Axis	Personal–emotional need
Work need	**Do not burden work with all the family needs; your spouse needs to help, too**
Work–family segment perceptions	– Work–family roles: Irrelevant – Work–family hierarchy: Both work spheres compromise and adjust to the meet family needs – Work–family mixture: Irrelevant
Family KSA	**Can use paid help when needed; cannot burden the spouse's work**
Work–family segment perceptions after fit synchronization	– Work–family roles: Irrelevant – Work–family hierarchy: Family compromises and adjusts to the work needs – Work–family mixture: Irrelevant

WFTS Exercise

Triangle of Life

Practice for All Stakeholders: Managers, Employees and Spouses

Design your WFTS triaxial contract using the following guide. This should be a continual process of many synchronization discussions in different settings. As noted, it takes several iterations to make sure everyone is synchronized, thinks they can make the necessary adjustments, and feels that their needs have been addressed, even if not entirely fulfilled. We provide templates for couple sync talks and work dyad sync talks. In the case of a triangle sync talk or manager–spouse sync talk, please adjust these templates accordingly.

Stage 1: Couple Dyad

1. Individually identify work and family needs
Man's perception of work (both workplaces) and family needs:

Functional–pragmatic needs	Relational needs	Personal–emotional needs

Woman's perception of work (both workplaces) and family needs:

Functional–pragmatic needs	Relational needs	Personal–emotional needs

2. Reflect on current work-family psychological contract
Reflect on your current couple work–family psychological contract. Have an open dialogue regarding how you, as a couple, operate the work–family interface. At this point, do not assess whether you are satisfied with the psychological contract. Only find out how you think things are going.

3. Synchronize the psychological contract segments

The needs reflect the three psychological contract segments. Use the mapped needs to discuss and synchronize the segments. First, extract the segment underlying each requirement. Next, discuss and sync the segments. Compare the segments you have now decided on, after mapping the needs, to those you reflected on at the beginning of the journey, as noted in Chapter 3.

Need	Work–family roles	Work–family hierarchy	Work–family mixture

Synchronized segments
Work–Family Roles

Please indicate how you want to manage the division of roles between you and your spouse:

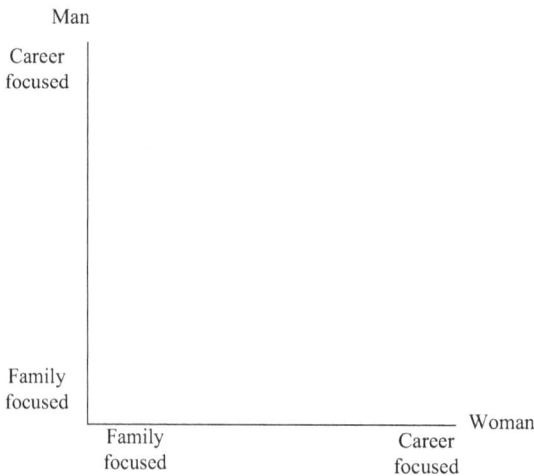

Man

Career
focused

Family
focused

Family   Career   Woman
focused   focused

Explain your choice:

_____

_____

_____

Work–Family Hierarchy

Please indicate how you want to manage the work–family hierarchy of your triangle system. Place points on the drawing that indicate the balance regarding who adjusts to whom. Mark two points, one in relation to the work of the woman and the other in relation to the work of the man.

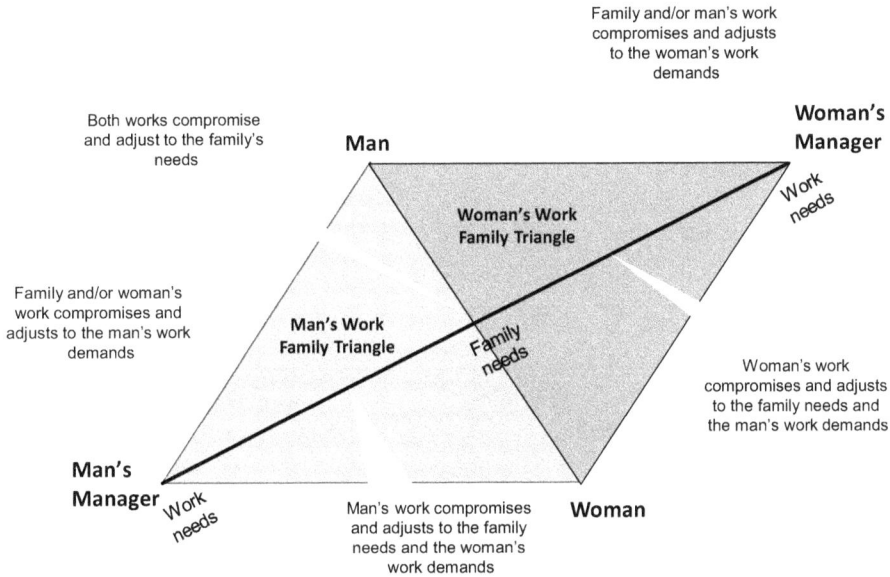

Explain your selection:

_____

_____

_____

Work–Family Mixture

Please indicate how you want to manage the interaction between work and family. Indicate the location of the man's work–family mixture and the woman's work–family mixture.

Man's work–family mixture:

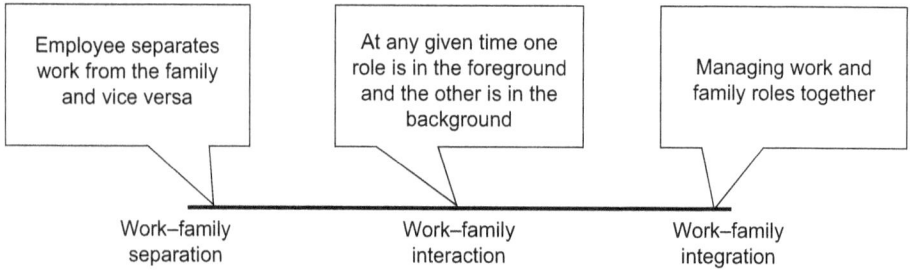

Employee separates work from the family and vice versa	At any given time one role is in the foreground and the other is in the background	Managing work and family roles together
Work–family separation	Work–family interaction	Work–family integration

Explain your selection:

_____

_____

_____

Woman's work–family mixture:

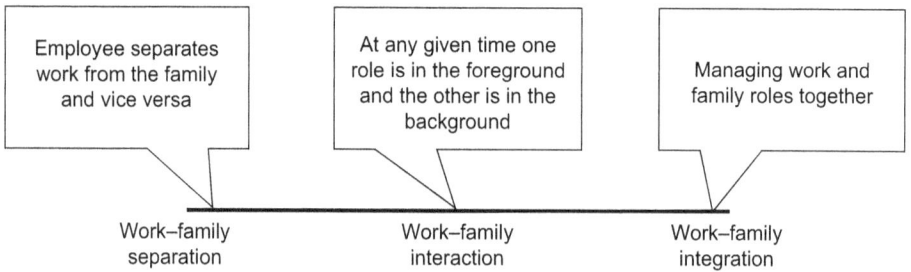

Employee separates work from the family and vice versa	At any given time one role is in the foreground and the other is in the background	Managing work and family roles together
Work–family separation	Work–family interaction	Work–family integration

Explain your selection:

_____

_____

_____

4. Synchronize needs

Go over the identified needs in light of the synchronized segments and discuss them. Understand what each one means and its significance. Prepare a synchronized list of work and family needs that you both see as legitimate needs that should be addressed.

Functional–pragmatic needs	Relational needs	Personal–emotional needs

5. Divide needs

Divide the needs into those that you can address as a couple and those that require the intervention of the manager.

Couple can address	Manager intervention needed

6. Meet needs

Discuss and find the proper way for you to address the needs that you can handle as a couple. Think of how you can use your KSA to meet the need.

Need	Axis (functional–pragmatic, relational, or personal–emotional)	KSA

7. Prioritize needs that require the intervention of the manager

Go over the needs that you feel you need the involvement of the manager (either the man's manager or the woman's manager) and prioritize them. Try to narrow the list and identify the five most important needs.

Needs to address with man's manager:

Prioritization	Need	Axis (functional–pragmatic, relational, or personal–emotional)
1		
2		
3		
4		
5		

Needs to address with woman's manager:

Prioritization	Need	Axis (functional–pragmatic, relational, or personal–emotional)
1		
2		
3		
4		
5		

Stage 2: Work Dyad

This stage is done with both the man's manager and the woman's manager. Each employee has to adjust the process according to their relationship with their manager.

1. Individually identify work and family needs

The employee already mapped the needs with their spouse. Before starting the sync talk, it is important that the manager identifies the work and family needs as they perceive them.

Functional–pragmatic needs	Relational needs	Personal–emotional needs

2. Reflection on current work-family psychological contract

Reflect on your current work–family psychological contract. Have an open dialogue regarding how you operate the work–family interface. At this point, do not assess whether you are satisfied with the psychological contract. Only find out how you think things are going.

3. Synchronize the psychological contract segments

The needs reflect the three psychological contract segments. Use the mapped needs to discuss and synchronize the segments. First, extract the segment underlying each requirement. Next, discuss and sync the segments. As a work dyad, the two segments that are relevant for the psychological contract are the work–family hierarchy and the work–family mixture.

Need	Work–family hierarchy	Work–family mixture

Synchronized segments
Work–Family Hierarchy

Please indicate how you want to manage the work–family hierarchy.

Family compromises and adjusts to the work needs	Work and family compromise and adjust to meet the other sphere needs	Work compromises and adjusts to the family needs

Work needs   Family needs

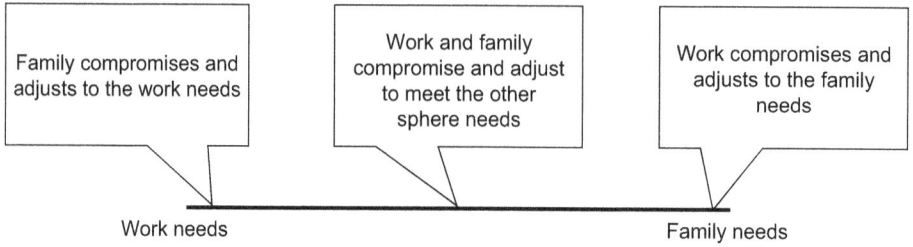

Explain your selection:

_____

_____

_____

Work–Family Mixture

Please indicate how you want to manage the interaction between work and family.

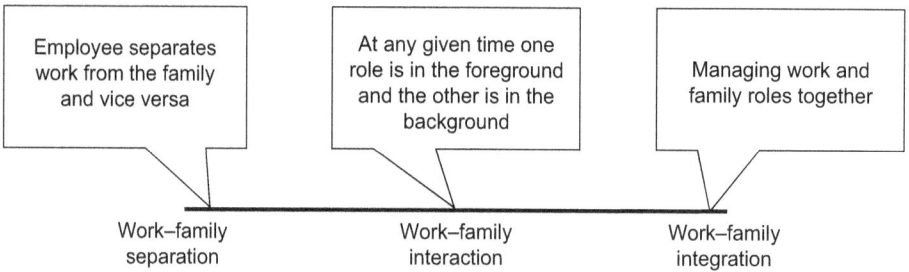

Employee separates work from the family and vice versa	At any given time one role is in the foreground and the other is in the background	Managing work and family roles together

Work–family separation   Work–family interaction   Work–family integration

Explain your selection:

_____

_____

_____

_____

_____

4. Synchronize needs

Go over the identified needs in light of the synchronized segments and discuss them. Understand what each one means and its significance. Prepare a synchronized list of work and family needs that you both see as legitimate needs that should be addressed.

Functional–pragmatic needs	Relational needs	Personal–emotional needs

5. Meet needs

Discuss and find the proper way for you to address the need. Think of how you can use your KSA to meet the need.

Need	Axis (functional–pragmatic, relational, or personal–emotional)	KSA

References

Caplan, R. D. (1987). Person-environment fit theory and organizations: Commensurate dimensions, time perspectives, and mechanisms. *Journal of Vocational Behavior, 31*(3), 248–267.

Diener, E. D., Emmons, R. A., Larsen, R. J., & Griffin, S. (1985). The Satisfaction with Life Scale. *Journal of Personality Assessment, 49*(1), 71–75.

Dolan, S. L. (2011). *Coaching by values (CBV): A guide to success in the life of business and the business of life*. iUniverse.

Edwards, J. R., & Van Harrison, R. (1993). Job demands and worker health: Three-dimensional reexamination of the relationship between person environment fit and strain. *Journal of Applied Psychology, 78*(4), 628–648.

Farrell, D. (1983). Exit, voice, loyalty, and neglect as responses to job dissatisfaction: A multidimensional scaling study. *Academy of Management Journal, 26*(4), 596–607.

Hirschman, A. O. (1970). *Exit, voice, and loyalty: Responses to decline in firms, organizations, and states*. Harvard University Press.

Chapter 7
Building and Developing a Trust Triangle Relationship

> You must trust and believe in people or life becomes impossible.
> – Anton Chekhov

The meaning of trust becomes clear when we try to imagine a world without trust. In such a world, we are exposed to manipulative leaders and individuals who are less committed to goals with chronic suspicions and of course, fear of interdependence. In such a world, a pragmatic position in any business interaction is to be shifty and tricky because otherwise you may find yourself on the losing side. The result may be that individuals place impermeable walls around them and thus, harm themselves as well. On the other hand, a world where trust is encouraged leads people to use a different lens. This lens offers the ability to see others not as rivals, to see what people have in common and not their differences, to experience the positive and not the negative, to give of yourself and not be guarded and defended, and to be cooperative instead of competitive in social situations (Deutsch, 1962). Such a world gives us the opportunity to compete morally and ethically and sometimes in cooperation with competitors, creating coopetition. Such a reality rises from the capacity of trust to serve as a mechanism for reducing uncertainty (Gao et al., 2005; Krishnan et al., 2016), a substitute for formal contracts, and an alternative to control mechanisms (Das & Teng, 1998). Trust serves as a coordination mechanism (Bradach & Eccles, 1989) and leads to effective interpersonal relationships (Larzelere & Huston, 1980). Therefore, during the last few decades, trust has become a key concept in social and organizational arenas. Researchers and practitioners use trust to explain human behaviors in daily life. As a result, many models explain how trust emerges, its significant role in how we interpret others' actions, and our resulting behavior.

Despite the frequent and common use of the term, trust is a complex concept that takes a different character in different circumstances. Yet there are characteristics common to most meanings, descriptions, and definitions. Tzafrir and Dolan (2004) argued that trust involves three principal concepts: vulnerability (Currall & Judge, 1995), reciprocity (Zand, 1972), and expectation (Lewicki & Bunker, 1996). Drawing on this research, they defined trust as a willingness to increase resource investment in another party based on positive expectations resulting from past positive mutual interactions (p. 116). This definition applies to all interactions in human life in which trust is involved, capturing its dynamic nature. These interactions occur at the macro (society) level and depend on the degree of trust of an individual in social institutions such as political, justice, education, and health systems, which affects, among other things, the willingness of individuals to get vaccinated during an epidemic. Other interactions are related to the meso level and include the level of trust of an individual in different reference groups; for example, the trust that employees have

https://doi.org/10.1515/9783110759808-007

in their human resources management system. And finally, they occur on the individual level, involving interactions that manifest in individual's relationships with other individuals (dyadic) in the workplace – for example, coworkers, subordinate managers – and continuing in the social system closest to the person and of course, in his or her home. These relationships do not work separately and often interact with each other. Therefore, it is important to understand the fabric of trust relationships in the overall context of the situation, country, culture, profession, organization, family, and individual (Fulmer & Gelfand, 2012).

It is important to understand that people can assign different meanings and weight to trust according to the context in which the interaction takes place (Zand, 1972). Individuals also have different tendencies to trust strangers, professionals, coworkers, and family members. Hence, the first meeting between two strangers, who will also meet in the future, is also a meeting point of two bases of initial trust. These dispositions can move across a continuum between high initial trust and low initial trust. This first encounter between individuals and the beginning of their interactions also reflects a sequence that ranges from match to mismatch regarding the initial trust of each participant. Figure 7.1 shows a large gap between the initial trust levels of two players. A point of departure can represent a case in which the greater the gap between the players, the greater the risk, the greater the intensity of positive interactions, and the more time it will take to create trust in such a dyad. In our example (Figure 7.1), this encounter involves a high level of suspicion and nervousness for Player B in the initial encounter, which can be changed in light of the actions of Player A.

Further regarding this disposition, the actions and reactions of the individuals can, as a rule, lead to a positive or negative cycle of trust. These cycles reflect an autocatalytic process, a process that strengthens itself. If there is a positive cycle, the gaps will narrow and may, over time, create harmony and respect between the players, and vice versa. A negative cycle will lead to increased suspicion, nervousness, and hostility between the players. Such occasions reflect a more general question: What important factors lead one player to trust another player?

Many studies have examined trustworthiness and suggested up to 10 factors that lead individuals to trust other individuals. For example, Mayer and colleagues (1995) argued that ability, benevolence, and integrity are the main domains of trustworthiness, whereas Mishra (1996) noted four components: skill, openness, concern, and reliability. Butler (1991) argued that 10 aspects lead people to trust others. Tzafrir and Dolan (2004), who examined the issue in the work context, concluded that three main dimensions exist: harmony, reliability, and concern (HRC). Studies around the globe have used Tzafrir and Dolan's (2004) conceptualization (Holtgrave et al., 2020; Rademaker et al., 2016; Sancho et al., 2018), dimensions, and scale in various countries such as Spain (Cabrera-Suárez et al., 2015; Mach et al., 2010), Portugal (Sousa et al., 2014), Hungary, the United Kingdom (More & Tzafrir, 2009), and New Zealand (Brien et al., 2015) and compared this scale to other scales (Dietz & Den Hartog, 2006; Laeequddin et al., 2010). These studies indicated a concept that applies to numerous industries,

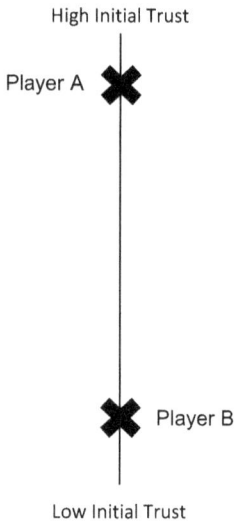

High Initial Trust

Player A ✖

✖ Player B

Low Initial Trust   **Figure 7.1:** Initial encounter and trust.

various interactions (for example, between employee and employer, organization and suppliers, and coach and team members), and different cultures.

How can trust be leveraged via HRC? Tzafrir and Dolan (2004, p. 127) suggested that concern is related to trust in terms of having a positive orientation toward others when interpreting their motives and behaving ethically. By doing so, the individual follows the principle of the golden rule: Do unto others as you would have them do unto you. Reliability refers to "systematic and consistent procedures and behaviors" that build and develop confidence in expectations about consistency between the words and actions of the party to be trusted (Rotter, 1980). Both dimensions capture the relationship and knowledge based the other party. Finally, harmony is a mixture of affect and identification regarding the other party, wherein a combination of abilities, feelings, opinions, purposes, and values inside the relationship exists. Harmony integrates the tangible and intangible and accomplishments, such as inaugurating a shared path, developing and understanding mutual goals, and engaging in social values.

The impact of each dimension is not identical and depends on the context in which the encounter between parties takes place (Branzei et al., 2007; Zenger & Folkman, 2019). Therefore, even when it comes to the same parties, the overall level of trust may vary and depend on the context, such as meeting in a workplace, university, hospital, or store, as well as the people involved: manager, coworker, family member, etc. For instance, Zenger and Folkman (2019) focused on leadership and projected consistency as the most important element. Accordingly, we suggest that in any situation, each side has to synchronize its behaviors according to other's characteristics, when the event takes place, the stage and length of the relationship, the power dynamics, and the magnitude of the situation at stake. When trust between players exists, it represents the undertaking of a risky course of action with the confident expectation that all players will act loyally, professionally, and respectfully.

In general, we tend to trust people we value and perceive to have moral characteristics (integrity and friendship), personal talents (knowledge, skills, abilities, and emotional intelligence), and social abilities (teamwork and awareness of others). Specifically, in organizations we look for managers with integrity, concern, empathy, and fairness; concerned colleagues; and subordinates with ability and integrity. Where the building blocks of such characteristics are strong, these aspects flourish and congruence can be achieved.

Trust and Work

The level of trust between parties determines their reactions to each event and situation, in part because individuals attribute different meaning to an action done by someone they trust compared to an individual they do not trust. For example, if I have a high level of trust in my manager and he asks me to stay late because he needs my help, I will interpret his request as a statement that he has confidence in me in terms of both professionalism and dedication, and I will willfully respond to the request. If I do not trust him, I might interpret the same request as his indifference to the fact that I have stayed late all week and see him as exploiting my devotion. In this case, I might give an excuse that explains why I cannot stay. These responses strengthen or weaken the cycle of trust. However, trust is not permanent and of course, certain actions taken over time may fracture or reinforce the relationship between the parties.

Figure 7.2 illustrates the interface between the world of work and the world of family. The dots and stars indicate actions that take place in each sphere. The dots are work actions and the stars are family actions. Many actions that occur in one sphere are not related to the other sphere and therefore, the intensity of their effect on the relationship with the other sphere is low. Other actions have a low, medium, or high impact on the other sphere, named work interference with family and family interference with work. Figure 7.2 also shows the space of discretion in which both parties will not react negatively to actions that may seemingly create conflict in one party between the spheres, and at its center is a state of equilibrium. The space of discretion represents, metaphorically, the ability of each party to move, without a sense of crisis, in this space in light of the fact that various events from the family sphere diffuse to the work sphere, and vice versa.

This space is not constant and stable; it varies from one employee to another employee, depending on the situation and of course, the level of trust between the parties. The result is a flexible and dynamic space that shrinks and expands according to the level of trust between the parties. Specifically, the higher the level of trust, the wider the space of discretion, and the lower the level of trust, the narrower the space. In daily life, each person performs many meaningful actions for and in each sphere.

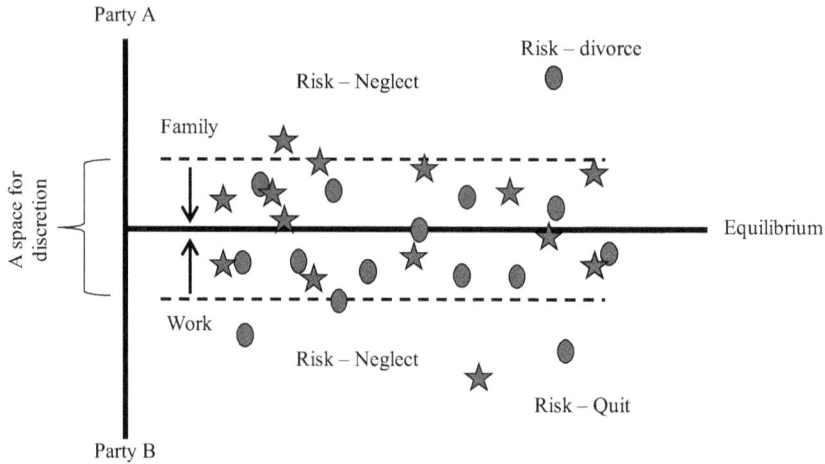

Figure 7.2: A space of discretion and trust.

Most of these behaviors are tied only to the relevant sphere or slightly connected to the other sphere. Yet some actions penetrate beyond the grid and diffuse between spheres, as does the risk that accompanies them. That is, the deeper the action falls in its sphere, the less risk there is for the other sphere. The closer the action is to the center of the horizontal axis, a medium level of risk of conflict exists, but for the most part, it is accountable and allows an equilibrium between spheres. When an action and its consequences cross the equilibrium line into the other sphere, risk is generated and the dilemma of how to respond occurs. Of paramount importance is crossing the line of discretion into the other sphere. This will act as a trigger for a significant response from the other player. An individual's action or behavior that is beyond the space of discretion can lead to a corresponding reaction that can deteriorate the situation to the point of leaving work or divorce at home.

> In the psychological contract of Dan and Tammy, weekends were out of the discretion space; there was no legitimacy for working on weekends, even in exceptional cases. During the week, Tammy had full discretion for deciding when she should work, even after usual hours, due to work needs, and Dan respected these situations even when there were busy periods and she arrived home late. It was important to Dan that weekends be protected from the entry of work into family life. After several incidents in which Tammy went to the office on the weekends to address issues that arose in the systems for which she was responsible, Dan informed her that either she was leaving the job and moving to a job that knew how to respect her private time or he was leaving. He could not go on like this. He felt he had to fight for time with her and that he was losing the war.

Figure 7.3 shows the differences between two cycles of trust: a situation where a high level of trust (dotted line) exists between the parties and a situation where a low level of trust (full line, plaid space) exists between the parties. In a situation with a high level of trust, more actions are contained by each party. In these cases, the psychological contract consists of guiding principles out of an understanding that each party

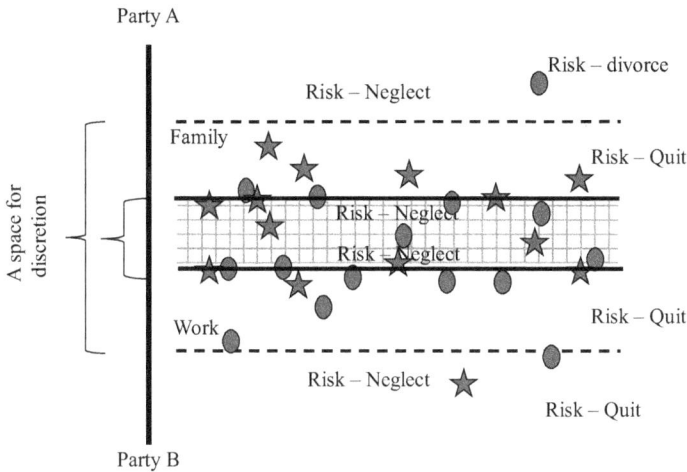

Figure 7.3: Discretion space depending on level of trust.

comes with good intentions and wants everyone to be satisfied. Consequently, all parties can synchronize their activities in coopetition.

In a situation with a low level of trust exists, almost any situation can lead to a conflict. As noted, one party subjectively perceives events and actions involving the other party differently, whether the level of trust is high or low. For example, consider a manager's request to work overtime. When harmony, reliability, and concern (trust) exist between parties, employees will perceive the request as justified and make a great effort in the direction of the manager, including talking with their spouse because they know their manager took their interests into account before requesting overtime work. When a low level of harmony, reliability, and concern (trust) exists, employees will act differently and feel great anger at their manager because they sense that their interests were not considered when the overtime decision was made. In these cases, when the level of trust is low, the psychological contract must be detailed and clear to allow for conduct with limited discretion. Players do not trust that the other party comes with good intentions and wants everyone to be satisfied. This does not allow the flexibility required to manage a work and family interface and makes the psychological contract more rigid to the point of being seen as a legal contract. Understanding this suggests that all players must build trust to increase the space of discretion.

Measuring and Developing Trust in the Working Environment

As demonstrated, when work and family interact, one is in focus and the other is pushed back. Such situations require organizations to improve employee well-being due to concern regarding the intensity of the psychological conflict that may occur. To implement a positive psychological contract, a system based on trust and respect must be achieved among stakeholders involved. Trust as glue in any social relationship helps the triangle manage the triad relationship. Tzafrir and Dolan's (2004) trust-ME model helps develop a trust triangle relationship that will enable the fulfillment of the WFTS psychological contract. Therefore, it is in organizations' and families' interest to implement HRC's underlying dimensions of trust into the work–family context.

How will individuals know how to behave and where to focus their efforts? Using our modified questionnaire based on Tzafrir and Dolan's (2004) measurement, they can determine their space of discretion. This modification (see WFTS Exercise in the end of the chapter) allows the manager, employee, and spouse to assess their situation across three trust dimensions and thus, more fruitfully manage their WFTS psychological contract.

Sixteen statements were based on a 5-point Likert scale ranging from 1 (*disagree strongly*) to 5 (*agree strongly*). Each questionnaire in the WFTS Exercise, identifies a specific referent – the trust target – and distinguishes among alternative targets. Our measurement distinguishes among manager, employee, and spouse and allows each stakeholder to assess their point of view. After answering the trust questionnaire, users should mark the scores on the trust web (see Figure 7.4) then connect the HRC dimension scores to create a "trust triangle." Managers should recognize that each team member's work–family triangle involves unique values, psychological contract, and trust triangle and thus, requires distinctive attention.

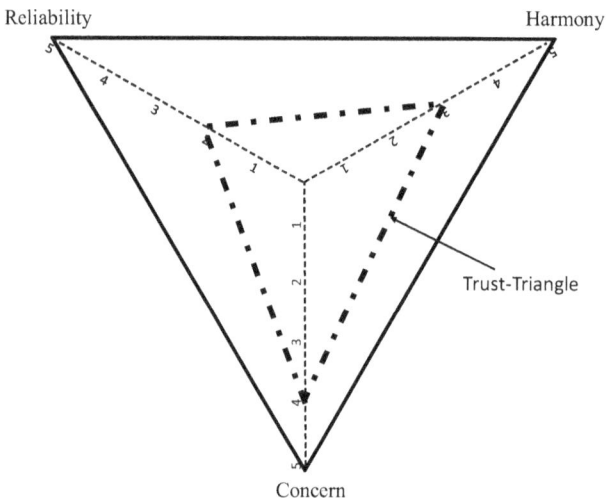

Figure 7.4: Trust web.

The use of this measurement enables stakeholders to track the level of trust in each triangle, and managers can evaluate the level of trust in their team. By asking respondents to indicate their perception of the level of trust in various dyads, managers can reveal key challenges or weaknesses that prevent the delivery of high employee performance. Accordingly, managers can take appropriate actions to improve or maintain aspects of trust. By so doing, they pay attention to relationships that are essential to WFTS and screen how each relationship is organized in a somewhat unique context, allowing them to reach wide-ranging insights about this triangle. Yet identifying the HRC dimensions of trust in a specific context requires more concentration on additional aspects in which they occur (deadlines, managing diversity, assessments, promotions, vacations, etc.).

Events that include clear procedures, regular operations, and especially scheduling of operations in one sphere only at the exact hours related to that sphere usually involve low risk. Therefore, trust plays a small role, and the space of discretion is less relevant. In these situations (stable and clear), the most projecting dimension is reliability, and other trust dimensions (concern and harmony) are considered less. Increasingly complex and uncertain events require flexibility and lead stakeholders to concentrate and rely on trust; thus, a wider space of discretion is necessary. Therefore, in such situations, an integrative understanding of the level of trust necessitates harmony and concern between stakeholders.

In summary, determining results can be done in two ways, depending on the context of the parties. A simple calculation of averages in each dimension involves summing the points for each statement and dividing by the number of statements. This action is adequate and gives a satisfactory point of view when it comes to a simple relationship in which the processes are modest without severe implications for family or work spheres, such as working fixed hours (9 a.m.–5 p.m.) with a fixed salary and without having to work unplanned overtime or when at home. In such a situation, it is possible to calculate the mean of each dimension and the total mean of trust because the interactions are known in advance with low complexity and no surprises. In these situations, the reliability dimension is more essential than harmony and concern. But when reliability is low, harmony and concern can compensate.

At the same time, more complex situations exist in work and many jobs cannot be separated between work and family spheres. Working hours cannot be demarcated. In these cases, no single dimension can hold the trust system. These situations require considering the multiple interactions between HRC dimensions, and a different method of calculation is vital. We can calculate the "trust interactions" by multiplying the three HRC dimensions. The number can range from 1 to 125. As we get closer to 125, the level of trust is higher between parties, representing an extraordinary space of discretion. The smaller the results, the narrow the space of discretion.

Who fills out the questionnaire? It is important that the questionnaires are filled out by each relevant stakeholder. That is, the manager, employee, and spouse should fill out a questionnaire for every trust target. All six results should be uploaded to the WFTS trust web (see Figure 7.5). The web allows stakeholders to see a visual image and examine gaps between the trust triangles.

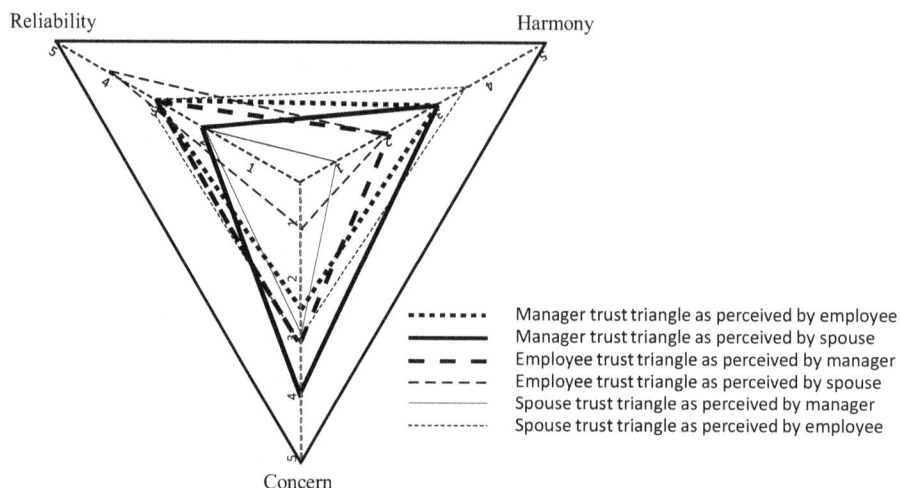

Figure 7.5: WFTS trust web.

Observing gaps in the trust web can be done in two ways. First, we observe the six trust triangles, as we see in Figure 7.5, and elaborate on the gaps. A gap that should be treated as critical is when the difference between respondents is greater than 10%. In those cases, we should analyze both the trust triangle and trust interactions and examine ways to reduce the gap. After observing the target trust web, we can calculate the work–family trust by summing all six trust interactions of the three stakeholders and dividing the number by six. The work–family trust range is between 1 and 125.

Figure 7.6 highlights the trust cycle, representing the space of discretion for each work–family triangle. For clarity, we present only three categories of triangle trust: low, modest, and high trust. In the first circle, a low level of trust exists among the three stakeholders, with a narrow space of discretion characterized by a state of low confidence, openness, and concern in the triangle. Thus, all sides will behave with cautiousness through maximum attention and constrain any action that may lead to a confrontation between dyads. The second circle reflects a state of modest trust and therefore, a wider space of discretion. In this situation, stakeholders maintain a well-structured relationship in common situations but face difficulty in complex situations that require flexibility and mutual concessions. Such relationships require constant reinforcement and synchronization among the parties to preserve the separate spheres' dyadic psychological contract. The third circle illustrates a high level of trust among the three stakeholders and consequently, a wider space of discretion. This case illustrates a situation where stakeholders share similar values that allow synchronization between actions in one sphere that require concessions in the second sphere in a way that does not lead to conflict and is done out of understanding and consideration. The ability of stakeholders to implement synchronization according to the relevant

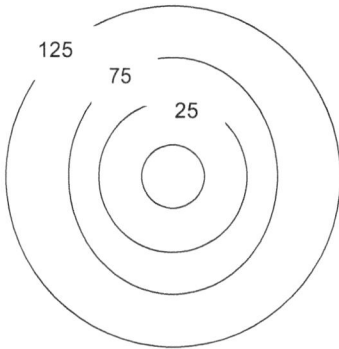

Figure 7.6: Trust cycle.

needs and time of each sphere leads to strengthening the cycle of trust following by an integrated triangle psychological contract – a WFTS psychological contract.

According to our model, we can anticipate what will happen between couples in the same scenario involving an urgent need to work after working hours on account of a joint plan. Let's assume an employee has a psychological contract with their spouse that work is important and only when the couple has set plans do they not work overtime. This case will help us understand the difference between the second and third circles of trust. In the second circle, a conflict will form in the couple if work interferes with planned family time, because their contract features a narrow space of discretion regarding this point. On the other hand, in the third circle, where trust has created a wider space of discretion, the result may be momentary anger that will pass quickly. That is, the higher the trust, the wider the space of discretion and therefore, the weaker the rigidity of the psychological contract, allowing more flexibility among the parties involved.

In summary, the trust web helps us respond to simple and common actions that represent events and their consequences, for which work and family can be easily distinguished. The trust cycle helps us respond to complex events and actions involving uncertainty and incorporate diverse values. It is essential to remember that each party has an initial tendency to trust another person in general and in specific situations. This basic understanding is the starting point of any relationship. If there is nothing at stake, then the term trust is not required. Only when the issue of investing resources in another party leads to the possibility of being impaired does trust hold great implications. In situations where the issue of trust is significant, cognitive and emotional processes can lead to a reaction, and vice versa. Two interesting and complex cases that combine uncertainty and high probability and involve trust and work–family issues are generational diversity and multinational firms. The case of multinational firms and global businesses as well as generational diversity – for example, expatriation and repatriation processes in multinational corporations or managerial relationships involving generational diversity – require even more attention from the employer regarding family issues.

Multinational Firms and Generational Diversity

Israel provides researchers and practitioners with a convenient laboratory for studying and analyzing advanced management practices, because it is a "maduradam" (microcosm) of the developed countries in Western Europe and North America (Harel & Tzafrir, 1999).

One organizational challenge rises from generational diversity, such as the intersection between managers leading a team composed of members from different generations. Knowing how to handle such diversity may lead to improvement; however, failing to do so may lead to loss. People from the same age group will tend to have more in common with each other with respect to norms, values, experiences, and topics of conversation, such as family issues. Lack of understanding of family issues can lead to conflicting events with no negative intention to do so. For instance, a young, single manager is not always aware of family commitments and requirements. The greater the age diversity in the team, the greater the likelihood of social disintegration. Therefore, working on increasing trust will help achieve a wider space of discretion, resulting in better communication and less interpersonal conflict.

A second organizational challenge is the need to balance national cultures with organizational culture, especially in multinational corporations. It is reasonable to assume that employees who grew up in different nations would have different world views, expectations, and values, resulting in different preferred approaches to communicating and interacting with others. Such a situation is multifaceted, and uncertainty can arouse many emotions. Expatriation and repatriation processes involving moving family members to a country with a different culture require boundless attention from the human resources management department. This can be achieved at the organizational level through training, socialization, and help with renting an apartment, finding a job for the spouse, and finding a school for the children. Beyond that, at the internal organizational level – involving individuals and teams – special attention is necessity. Human resources management departments can use our model to understand what can and should be emphasized to build trust. Trust allows us to cope more easily in such a dual world in a way that eases uncertainty and allows expatriates to socialize quickly, learn how to respond and react to activities, reduce doubt, and decrease negative feelings and judgments. That is, given that time is worth money, trust is essential for team and organizational efficiency and survival.

What have we learned so far? We have seen that trust is very important to our organizational and daily activities, especially in situations that are demanding and dynamic. We realized that trust is a multidimensional concept composed of harmony, reliability, and concern. Understanding trust mechanisms in the work–family triangle allows us to respond in a well-ordered and optimal way. In simple cases, we should focus only on the relevant dimensions, versus complex cases that require us to shape a holistic view, using our six-step model. In the first step, we need to understand the challenge and circumstances in the specific context. The second step is to collect questionnaires from all participants involved in each work–family triangle. The third step is calculating and analyzing the results according to the specific situation, then planning actions that match the challenges depending on the stakeholders. The fourth step is implementation with a timetable, concentrating on building trust that leads to WFTS. The fifth step is examining how the circumstances are progressing at home and at work, followed by the sixth step, acquiring feedback from each stakeholder in the triangle.

New Concepts in the Chapter
- *Trust triangle* – The triangle formed as a result of connecting the scores of the three trust dimensions (harmony, reliability, and concern).
- *Trust interactions* – The result of multiplying the three trust dimensions, with a score that can range from 1 to 125.
- *Space of discretion* – An area where stakeholders have an increased probability of a positive reaction to undesirable actions or decisions because they all trust the good intentions of others even when the outcome is unattractive to one of them.

WFTS Exercise

Triangle of Life

The following are the trust questionnaires based on Tzafrir and Dolan's (2004) Trust ME Questionnaire. We recommend four steps to designing your WFTS trust web:

1. Each stakeholder (manager, employee, and spouse) should fill out a questionnaire for every trust target.
2. Calculate the questionnaire scores. Questions 8, 9, 14, 15, and 16 represent harmony dimension in the workplace and capture an amalgamation of each player's perceptions of their abilities and personal relationships as a sense of shared principles and unity. Questions 1, 6, 7, 11, and 12 represent reliability and measure the players' perceptions, consistency, and obligation to one another. The third dimension, concern, is composed from Questions 2, 3, 4, 5, 10, and 13 and represents respondents' perceptions of how an employee's or manager's "self-interest is balanced by interest in the welfare of others" (Mishra, 1996, p. 267).
3. Mark the average score for each dimension on the trust web and then connect the HRC dimension scores to create a "trust triangle."
4. All six results should be placed in the trust web. Use a different color for each triangle. This is the WFTS trust web. The WFTS trust web allows stakeholders to see a visual image and examine gaps among trust triangles. Reflect on the gaps and their implications and design the way you want, as a co-opetition triangle, to handle things and build a better trust system.

Manager

Dear manager, think about your employee. Indicate the degree to which you agree with each statement using the following scale.

1	2	3	4	5
Disagree strongly	Disagree	Neither agree nor disagree	Agree	Agree strongly

1. My needs and desires are very important to them.	
2. I can count on them to help me if I have difficulties with my job.	
3. They would not knowingly do anything to hurt me.	
4. They are open and up front with me.	
5. I think that they succeed by stepping on other people. (reverse coded)	

6. They will keep the promises they make.	
7. They really look out for what is important to me.	
8. They have a lot of knowledge about the things that needs to be done.	
9. They are known to be successful in the things they attempt to accomplish.	
10. If I make a mistake, they are willing to forgive and forget.	
11. Their actions and behaviors are not consistent. (reverse coded)	
12. They take actions that are consistent with their words.	
13. It is best not to share information with them. (reverse coded)	
14. There is a lot of warmth in the relationship between us.	
15. They would make personal sacrifices for me.	
16. They express their true feelings about important issues.	

If you know the employee's spouse at a certain level, indicate the degree to which you agree with each statement using the following scale.

1	2	3	4	5
Disagree strongly	Disagree	Neither agree nor disagree	Agree	Agree strongly

1. My needs and desires are very important to them.	
2. I can count on them to help me if I have difficulties with my job.	
3. They would not knowingly do anything to hurt me.	
4. They are open and up front with me.	
5. I think that they succeed by stepping on other people. (reverse coded)	
6. They will keep the promises they make.	
7. They really look out for what is important to me.	
8. They have a lot of knowledge about the things that needs to be done.	
9. They are known to be successful in the things they attempt to accomplish.	
10. If I make a mistake, they are willing to forgive and forget.	
11. Their actions and behaviors are not consistent. (reverse coded)	
12. They take actions that are consistent with their words.	
13. It is best not to share information with them. (reverse coded)	
14. There is a lot of warmth in the relationship between us.	
15. They would make personal sacrifices for me.	
16. They express their true feelings about important issues.	

For the two questionnaires, mark the average score for each dimension on the trust web and then connect the HRC dimension scores to create a "trust triangle." Use a different color for each triangle.

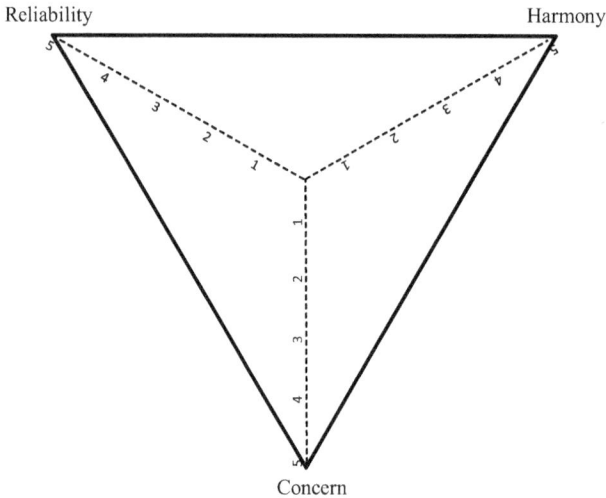

Reliability   Harmony

Concern

Employee

Dear employee, think about your manager. Indicate the degree to which you agree with each statement using the following scale.

1	2	3	4	5
Disagree strongly	Disagree	Neither agree nor disagree	Agree	Agree strongly

1. My needs and desires are very important to them.	
2. I can count on them to help me if I have difficulties with my job.	
3. They would not knowingly do anything to hurt me.	
4. They are open and up front with me.	
5. I think that they succeed by stepping on other people. (reverse coded)	
6. They will keep the promises they make.	
7. They really look out for what is important to me.	
8. They have a lot of knowledge about the things that needs to be done.	
9. They are known to be successful in the things they attempt to accomplish.	

10. If I make a mistake, they are willing to forgive and forget.	
11. Their actions and behaviors are not consistent. (reverse coded)	
12. They take actions that are consistent with their words.	
13. It is best not to share information with them. (reverse coded)	
14. There is a lot of warmth in the relationship between us.	
15. They would make personal sacrifices for me.	
16. They express their true feelings about important issues.	

Think about your spouse in the context of the work–family interface. Indicate the degree to which you agree with each statement using the following scale.

1	2	3	4	5
Disagree strongly	Disagree	Neither agree nor disagree	Agree	Agree strongly

1. My needs and desires are very important to them.	
2. I can count on them to help me if I have difficulties with my job.	
3. They would not knowingly do anything to hurt me.	
4. They are open and up front with me.	
5. I think that they succeed by stepping on other people. (reverse coded)	
6. They will keep the promises they make.	
7. They really look out for what is important to me.	
8. They have a lot of knowledge about the things that needs to be done.	
9. They are known to be successful in the things they attempt to accomplish.	
10. If I make a mistake, they are willing to forgive and forget.	
11. Their actions and behaviors are not consistent. (reverse coded)	
12. They take actions that are consistent with their words.	
13. It is best not to share information with them. (reverse coded)	
14. There is a lot of warmth in the relationship between us.	
15. They would make personal sacrifices for me.	
16. They express their true feelings about important issues.	

For the two questionnaires, mark the average score for each dimension on the trust web and then connect the HRC dimension scores to create a "trust triangle." Use a different color for each triangle.

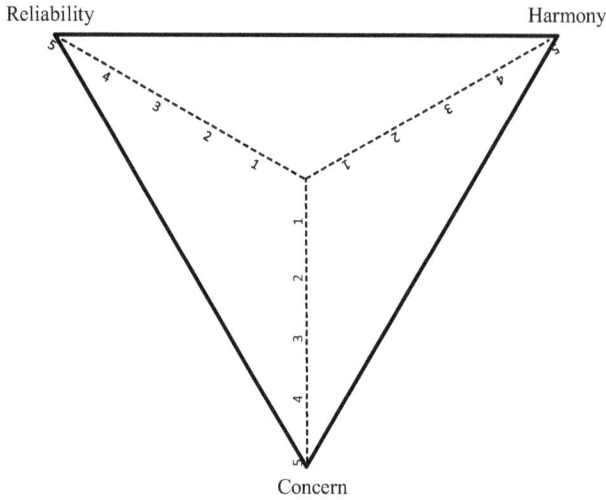

Reliability   Harmony

Concern

Spouse

Dear spouse, think about your spouse in the context of the work–family interface.
Indicate the degree to which you agree with each statement using the following scale.

1	2	3	4	5
Disagree strongly	Disagree	Neither agree nor disagree	Agree	Agree strongly

1. My needs and desires are very important to them.	
2. I can count on them to help me if I have difficulties with my job.	
3. They would not knowingly do anything to hurt me.	
4. They are open and up front with me.	
5. I think that they succeed by stepping on other people. (reverse coded)	
6. They will keep the promises they make.	
7. They really look out for what is important to me.	
8. They have a lot of knowledge about the things that needs to be done.	
9. They are known to be successful in the things they attempt to accomplish.	
10. If I make a mistake, they are willing to forgive and forget.	
11. Their actions and behaviors are not consistent. (reverse coded)	
12. They take actions that are consistent with their words.	
13. It is best not to share information with them. (reverse coded)	

14. There is a lot of warmth in the relationship between us.	
15. They would make personal sacrifices for me.	
16. They express their true feelings about important issues.	

Think about the employee's manager. Indicate the degree to which you agree with each statement using the following scale.

1	2	3	4	5
Disagree strongly	Disagree	Neither agree nor disagree	Agree	Agree strongly

1. My needs and desires are very important to them.	
2. I can count on them to help me if I have difficulties with my job.	
3. They would not knowingly do anything to hurt me.	
4. They are open and up front with me.	
5. I think that they succeed by stepping on other people. (reverse coded)	
6. They will keep the promises they make.	
7. They really look out for what is important to me.	
8. They have a lot of knowledge about the things that needs to be done.	
9. They are known to be successful in the things they attempt to accomplish.	
10. If I make a mistake, they are willing to forgive and forget.	
11. Their actions and behaviors are not consistent. (reverse coded)	
12. They take actions that are consistent with their words.	
13. It is best not to share information with them. (reverse coded)	
14. There is a lot of warmth in the relationship between us.	
15. They would make personal sacrifices for me.	
16. They express their true feelings about important issues.	

For the two questionnaires, mark the average score for each dimension on the trust web and then connect the HRC dimension scores to create a "trust triangle." Use a different color for each triangle.

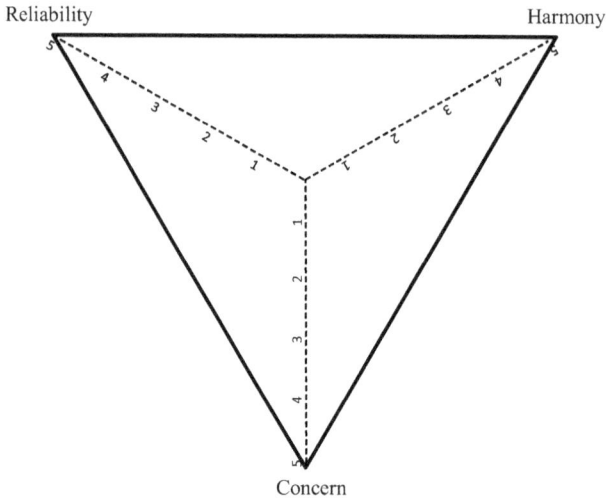

The WFTS trust web

Please add all six results to the trust web. Each respondent should be marked in a different color. The web allows you to see a visual image and examine gaps among trust triangles. Reflect on the gaps and their implications and design the way you want, as a co-opetition triangle, to handle things and build a better trust system.

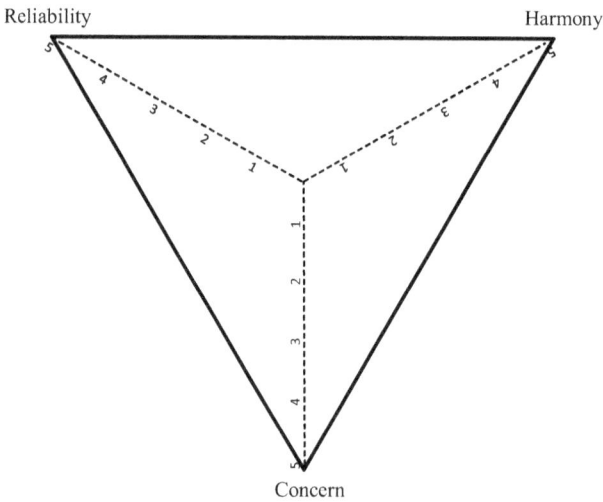

References

Bradach, J. L., & Eccles, R. G. (1989). Price, authority, and trust: From ideal types to plural forms. *Annual Review of Sociology*, *15*(1), 97–118.

Branzei, O., Vertinsky, I., & Camp, R. D., II. (2007). Culture-contingent signs of trust in emergent relationships. *Organizational Behavior and Human Decision Processes*, *104*(1), 61–82.

Brien, A., Thomas, N., & Hussein, A. S. (2015). Turnover intention and commitment as part of organizational social capital in the hotel industry. *Journal of Human Resources in Hospitality & Tourism*, *14*(4), 357–381.

Butler Jr, J. K. (1991). Toward understanding and measuring conditions of trust: Evolution of a conditions of trust inventory. *Journal of Management*, *17*(3), 643–663.

Cabrera-Suárez, M. K., Déniz-Déniz, M. C., & Martín-Santana, J. D. (2015). Family social capital, trust within the TMT, and the establishment of corporate goals related to nonfamily stakeholders. *Family Business Review*, *28*(2), 145–162.

Currall, S. C., & Judge, T. A. (1995). Measuring trust between organizational boundary role persons. *Organizational behavior and Human Decision processes*, *64*(2), 151–170.

Das, T. K., & Teng, B. S. (1998). Between trust and control: Developing confidence in partner cooperation in alliances. *Academy of Management Review*, *23*(3), 491–512.

Deutsch, M. (1962). Cooperation and trust: Some theoretical notes. In M. R. Jones (Ed.), *Nebraska Symposium on Motivation, 1962* (pp. 275–320). University of Nebraska Press.

Dietz, G., & Den Hartog, D. N. (2006). Measuring trust inside organisations. *Personnel Review*, *35*(5), 557–588.

Fulmer, C. A., & Gelfand, M. J. (2012). At what level (and in whom) we trust: Trust across multiple organizational levels. *Journal of Management*, *38*(4), 1167–1230.

Gao, T., Sirgy, M. J., & Bird, M. M. (2005). Reducing buyer decision-making uncertainty in organizational purchasing: Can supplier trust, commitment, and dependence help? *Journal of Business Research*, *58*(4), 397–405.

Harel, G. H., & Tzafrir, S. S. (1999). The effect of human resource management practices on the perceptions of organizational and market performance of the firm. *Human Resources Management*, *38*(3), 185–199.

Holtgrave, M., Nienaber, A. M., Tzafrir, S. S., & Schewe, G. (2020). Cooperation in the face of conflict: Effects of top managers' trust beliefs in their firms' major suppliers. *British Journal of Management*, *31*(2), 253–273.

Krishnan, R., Geyskens, I., & Steenkamp, J. B. E. (2016). The effectiveness of contractual and trust-based governance in strategic alliances under behavioral and environmental uncertainty. *Strategic Management Journal*, *37*(12), 2521–2542.

Laeequddin, M., Sahay, B. S., Sahay, V., & Waheed, K. A. (2010). Measuring trust in supply chain partners' relationships. *Measuring Business Excellence*, *14*(3), 53–69.

Larzelere, R. E., & Huston, T. L. (1980). The Dyadic Trust Scale: Toward understanding interpersonal trust in close relationships. *Journal of Marriage and the Family*, *42*(3), 595–604.

Lewicki, R.J., & Bunker, B.B. 1996. Developing and maintaining trust in work relationships. In M.R. Kramer & R.T. Tyler (Eds.), *Trust in organizations: Frontiers of theory and research*: 114–139. Thousand Oaks, CA: Sage.

Mach, M., Dolan, S., & Tzafrir, S. (2010). The differential effect of team members' trust on team performance: The mediation role of team cohesion. *Journal of Occupational and Organizational Psychology*, *83*(3), 771–794.

Mayer, R. C., Davis, J. H., & Schoorman, F. D. (1995). An integrative model of organizational trust. *Academy of Management Review*, *20*(3), 709–734.

Mishra, A.K. 1996. Organizational response to crisis: The centrality of trust. In M.R. Kramer & R.T. Tyler (Eds.), *Trust in organizations: Frontiers of theory and research*: 261–287. Thousand Oaks, CA: Sage

More, K. V., & Tzafrir, S. S. (2009). The role of trust in core team employees: A three-nation study. Cross Cultural Management, *16*(4), 410–433.

Rademaker, L. L., Duffy, J. O. C., Wetzler, E., & Zaikina-Montgomery, H. (2016). Chair perceptions of trust between mentor and mentee in online doctoral dissertation mentoring. *Online Learning*, *20*(1), 57–69.

Rotter, J. B. (1980). Interpersonal trust, trustworthiness, and gullibility. *American Psychologist*, *35*(1), 1–7.

Sancho, M. P. L., Martínez-Martínez, D., Jorge, M. L., & Madueño, J. H. (2018). Understanding the link between socially responsible human resource management and competitive performance in SMEs. *Personnel Review*, *47*(6), 1211–1243.

Sousa, S., Silva, I. S., Veloso, A., Tzafrir, S., & Enosh, G. (2014). Client's violence toward social workers. *Tékhne*, *12*, 69–78.

Tzafrir, S. S., and Dolan, L. S. (2004). Trust ME: A scale for measuring employee manager trust. *Management Research*: *The Journal of the Iberoamerican Academy of Management,* 2(2), 115 – 132.

Zand, D. E. (1972). Trust and managerial problem solving. *Administrative science quarterly*, 229–239.

Zenger, J., & Folkman, J. (2019). The 3 elements of trust. *Harvard Business Review*, *87*(2), 2–6

Summary

> In order to act differently, one must first learn to see the world differently.
> –Watzlawick (1987)

For many years, society has coped with the complex situation of two demanding spheres: the work sphere and the family sphere. In the past, society had a traditional answer regarding the "correct" way to manage this double-sphere situation. The traditional solution was to divide the spheres between the parents such that each parent is fully dedicated to one sphere and does not have to split their time, attention, and identity (Greenhaus & Powell, 2017). The man was typically the "breadwinner," the provider, focusing on his work, and the woman was typically the "homemaker," focusing on taking care of home tasks and raising children. However, core environmental changes occurred that shuffled the cards: (a) advancement of communication technologies created a 24/7 work environment; (b) the employment psychological contract changed from stable long-term settings to short-term unstable settings; (c) participation of women in the labor force increased; and (d) social changes toward gender equality and changes in the role assumed by fathers occurred.

Nowadays, society does not have an answer for this new setting, and the common understanding is that there is no way to truly manage the work–family interface satisfactorily. It seems like an unsolvable conflict, and one sphere is always sacrificing at expense of the other. It is a constant struggle, and there are always winners and losers. Most employees feel that in such a conflict, home is the main loser. In many workshops we conducted on this subject and several studies, the feeling is of despair and acceptance of such a decree. The feeling is that the choice is either accepting that one sphere will sacrifice for the other or a constant feeling of pressure at an expensive mental price. The following are some of the feelings we have been heard over years of studies and workshops:

- "It's discouraging. There will always be someone disappointed in me, either my manager or my spouse."
- "I'm in a constant race knowing I cannot win, only reduce damage."
- "In today's reality, I chose not to bring children. There is no way to pursue a career with a family without hurting someone."
- "Sometimes I miss how the things were in my parents' time. Everyone knew what their role was and there was no need to juggle all together."

After years of working with organizations and couples, we have come to a different conclusion. The interface can be managed in a healthy and optimal way, with work–family triangle synchronization (WFTS). As Watzlawick (1987) stated: "In order to act differently, one must first learn to see the world differently." Managing the work and family interface with WFTS requires changing four essential assumptions. Consultants, managers, employees, and family members must first modify their perceptions

https://doi.org/10.1515/9783110759808-008

regarding the interface. Then they can possess the tools with which they can manage the interface effectively. In this book, we detailed these four working assumptions and revealed how step by step, it is possible to design a healthy and realistic psychological contract to cope with interface challenges.

(a) The Triangle Interface

Understanding that the interface is a triangle of three players who all have a part in managing the interface is a significant perceptual revolution. WFTS recognizes that three main players handle daily aspects of the work and family interface: manager, employee, and spouse.[1] The players interact via three dyads: manager–employee, manager–spouse, and employee–spouse. Every player should be aware of the additional players who have the power to affect the system. The main point of blindness is that of the manager toward the spouse. The manager must understand the power of the spouse in the interface. In Chapter 3, we talked about the relationship-intensity spaces of the manager–spouse dyad. Managing this space and acknowledging the role of the spouse in the interface is the first step in designing a successful psychological contract. Next, as described in Chapter 4, the players have to understand the dynamics of a triangle relationship to manage their own triangle dynamics in a way that manages and resolves the dyads' tension rather than bypassing it through the third apex of the triangle.

(b) From Balance to Synchronization

In Chapter 5, we pointed out that WFTS changes the work–family interface goal from the familiar work–family balance to work–family synchronization. WFTS does not represent or assume an equal level of engagement in the two spheres, nor does it seek to balance the interactions as its goals; rather, WFTS focuses on synchronization depending on the specific context and precise time. Johns (2006) defined context as "situational opportunities and constraints that affect the occurrence and meaning of organizational behavior as well as functional relationships variables" (p. 386). The context of every work–family system in this new reality is unique. Every system has its variance in how it reacts to global, economic, and social changes. This leads to an inconsistent balance between the work and family. This balance varies between and within families regarding different periods in life and different contexts. The goal is to enable working individuals to cope with the different, dynamic, and complex

---

1 There are other important players like grandparents, children, and friends. However, the three players that the book focuses on are the main stakeholders, and they are the ones who mediate between work and family and the secondary stakeholders.

demands of work–family interfaces in which they act, looking for synchronization among the three players regarding the correct way for them to manage the work–family interface.

(c) Tailor Suit Synchronization

Understanding that each system has its unique needs and abilities and must synchronize its own fit is a key role. Our years of studies and workshops have shown that that no single solution suits all work–family triangle systems. Each triangle system has its own needs and abilities and therefore, its own tailored work–family fit. This is contrary to family-friendly programs. An example that illustrates the difference between a comprehensive response and a unique response is the phenomenon in which organizations name one day of the week – in many companies, it's Tuesdays or Thursdays – as a "family day" during which employees finish their work early. For many families, this is not the right day for them because of their specific personal circumstances. These families would enjoy such a family day; however, they would have preferred a different day. Once the organization has given this benefit, even though it is not good for the employees, they do not have the ability to get different knowledge, skills, or abilities (KSA) that will better suit their needs. The organization and managers need to build an HR process that enables stakeholders to clarify, settle, and shape their own unique solution, their own unique WFTS psychological contract. By synchronizing the needs and KSA of the work and family and how they want to handle them, the stakeholders can manage the conflict, improve the way they accomplish their work and family roles, and achieve well-being. Chapter 6 describes the WFTS triaxial contract design process.

(d) A Co-Opetiton Psychological Contract

Chapter 5 deals with work–family triangle power relationship. There are no losers and winners; the psychological contract must be managed in co-opetition. WFTS acknowledges that work and family are in constant conflict. Comparing the management of this conflict through competition as a "tug-of-war" or as a cooperative power relationship, we conclude that work and family conflict is not a power struggle with losers and winners. Instead, managing the interface with co-opetition can better meet the work–family interface challenge. To do so, the players must develop a trusting relationship. Chapter 7 details the way they can build, develop, and retain this relationship.

The contributions of this book are both conceptual and practical. Conceptually, recognizing that the work–family interface can be studied as a triangle system of three stakeholders can open the field to a new research area, revealing the sensitive, sometimes hidden dynamic between the unconventional dyads of the work and family interface: the indirect influence of the manager–spouse dyad and the indirect influence of the man's manager–woman's manager dyad in dual-earner families. "There is nothing more practical than a good theory" (Lewin, 1952, p. 169). WFTS, with its new concepts, also has a practical contribution: the WFTS triaxial psychological contract as detailed in Chapter 6. The following are examples, illustrated in Figures S.1 and S.2, demonstrating the same trigger resulting in two different dynamic patterns. The first example is a synchronized competition triangle power relationship and the second is a WFTS psychological contract, designed and managed in a co-opetition triangle power relationship.

In Figure S.1, the *work–family psychological contract* regarding working hours is not synchronized. The woman's manager thinks (out of sync with the employee) that it is acceptable to call her employee at 22:00 and ask her to work with her team. The wife and her husband are not synchronized as to whether the wife should comply by answering the call and doing the task the manager requested. This couple's unsynchronized fit is managed as a *tug-of-war triangle power relationship*. Each one pulls to another side. The man demands that the woman not comply, and the woman complies and creates *tension* in the couple dyad. The same tension occurs in the work dyad, but only on the woman's (employee's) side. She does not communicate and synchronize with her manager regarding her request; she complies with resentment and creates *tension* in the work dyad.

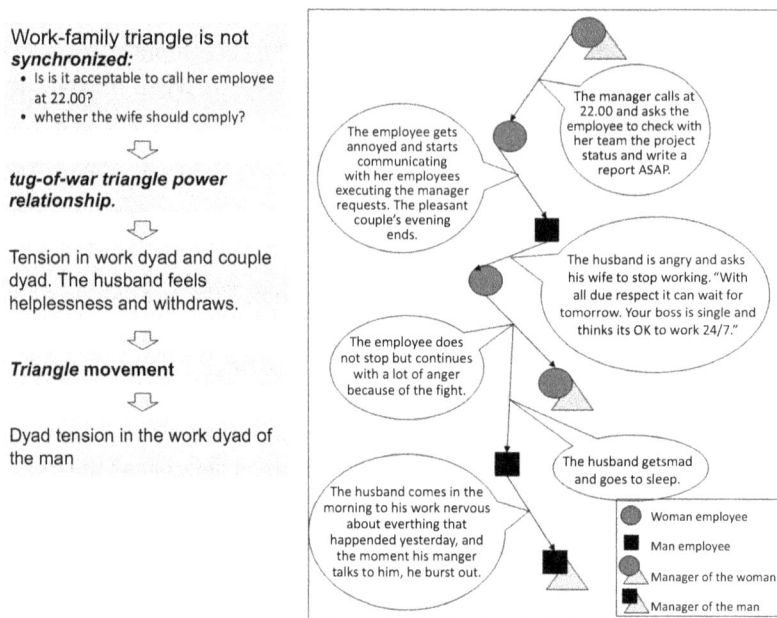

Work-family triangle is not synchronized:
- Is is it acceptable to call her employee at 22.00?
- whether the wife should comply?

⇩

tug-of-war triangle power relationship.

⇩

Tension in work dyad and couple dyad. The husband feels helplessness and withdraws.

⇩

***Triangle* movement**

⇩

Dyad tension in the work dyad of the man

The employee gets annoyed and starts communicating with her employees executing the manager requests. The pleasant couple's evening ends.

The manager calls at 22.00 and asks the employee to check with her team the project status and write a report ASAP.

The husband is angry and asks his wife to stop working. "With all due respect it can wait for tomorrow. Your boss is single and thinks its OK to work 24/7."

The employee does not stop but continues with a lot of anger because of the fight.

The husband getsmad and goes to sleep.

The husband comes in the morning to his work nervous about everthing that happended yesterday, and the moment his manger talks to him, he burst out.

- ⬤ Woman employee
- ◼ Man employee
- ◥ Manager of the woman
- ◢ Manager of the man

Figure S.1: Competition example of work–family triangle dynamic.

The husband feels *helplessness* about the *work–family psychological contract* and withdraws (*exit response*), creating a *triangle movement* (the members of the work dyad, the manager and employee, become closer at the expense of the couple dyad). This generates another *dyad tension* in the work dyad of the man. In summary, the *tug-of-war triangle power system management type* did not make it possible for the dyads to manage the conflict in a *co-opetition* manner that would have prevented this stress chain.

The second example, illustrated in Figure S.2, is a co-opetition triangle power relationship situation started by the same trigger. The *WFTS psychological contract* regarding working hours is synchronized. All three stakeholders agree that working at night is an exception (*harmony and concern trust dimensions*). The couple trusts the woman's manager, knowing that if she asks the woman to work at exceptional hours, it must be important (*reliability trust dimension*). The *triangle power relationship* is a *co-opetition management type*, where the three stakeholders understand the *need of the work* (an urgent status report) and the couple's needs (couple time at night) and synchronized these needs. The *satisfaction of these three stakeholders with the WFTS triaxial psychological contract* is between *adjustment* and *compromise*. The couple would prefer no phone calls at night but understands that in the case of this manager (the woman's manager), it is not possible (not included in her KSA). The manager prefers working at night after her children are asleep but understands the need of the couple for "couple time." Acknowledging that co-opetition management is the best way to manage competition at night, they decided that working at night is an exception.

In conclusion, it doesn't matter which of the three players (manager, employee, or spouse) you are, nor your personal position regarding the correct way to manage work–family conflict. What matters is your ability to synchronize with your triangle partners and make all partners feel that both spheres are being respectfully addressed.

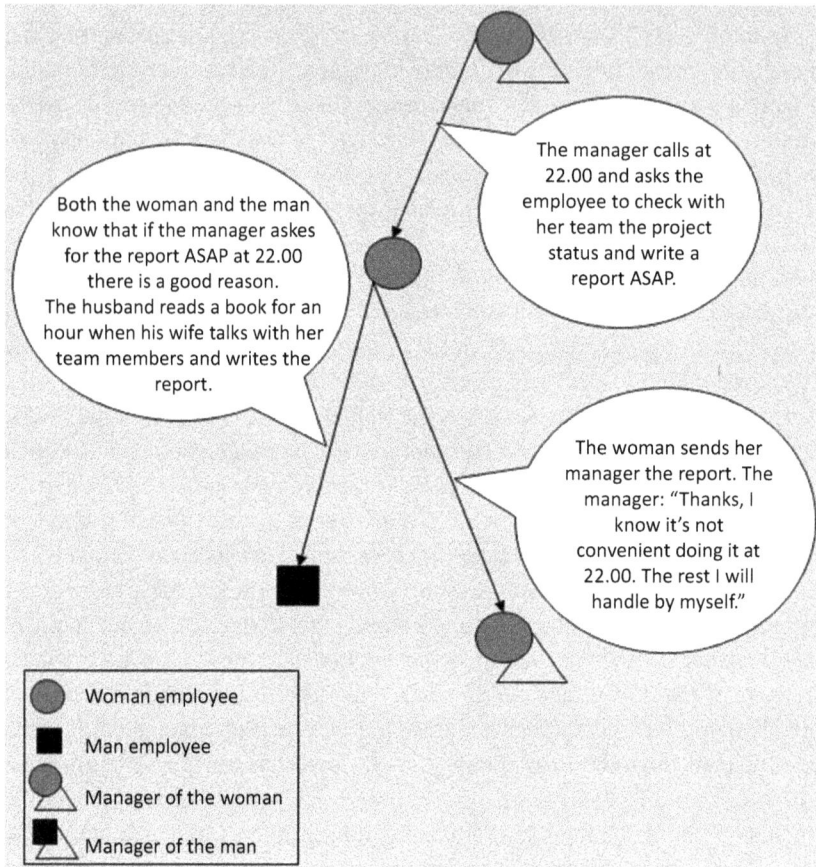

Figure S.2: Co-opetition example of work–family triangle dynamic.

References

Greenhaus, J. H., & Powell, G. N. (2017) *Making Work and Family Work: From hard choices to smart choices*. Routledge.

Johns, G. (2006). The essential impact of context on organizational behavior. *Academy of management review*, *31*(2), 386–408.

Lewin, K. (1952). *Field theory in social science: Selected theoretical papers by Kurt Lewin*. Tavistock.

Watzlawick, P. (1987). If you desire to see, learn how to act. In J. Zeig (Ed.), *The evolution of psychotherapy* (pp. 91–100). Brunner/Mazel.

List of Figures

https://doi.org/10.1515/9783110759808-009

.

List of Tables

https://doi.org/10.1515/9783110759808-010

About the Authors

Dr. Anat Garti is a social psychologist, couples and family therapist, management consultant, and coach. For the past decade, she has been training consultants and therapists for professional certification. She is a researcher and lecturer in three main fields: work–family conflict; stress, burnout, and resilience; and managing by values. She is the chief psychologist of the Israel Values Center and part of the clinical staff and teaching staff at Shinui Institute. Recently, she wrote a book with Prof. Simon Dolan titled *The Parent as an Anchor* and developed, with M.D.S. Zinquo and the Israel Values Center, the "Stress Map" – a gamification that enables a visual way to explore, evaluate, and execute the overall stress system. Contact: anatgarti@gmail.com

Prof. Shay Tzafrir focuses his research on people management and especially the interface among trust, human capital, and stakeholder behavior. He has been involved in training and development since 1989. Between 2016 and 2021, he served as the head of the Haifa School of Business Administration and director of the Center for Organizational Research and Human Resource Management. In 2016, he co-founded the *Quarterly for Organizational Research and Human Resource Management*, a journal dedicated to the contributions of academic research to the business and public community of Israel. Throughout the years, he has held numerous positions at the university: senate member, member of the University Constitution Committee, and more. At the public level, he was the chairman of the Israeli Industrial Relations Research Association (2009–2011) and a lay judge at the Israeli National Labor Court (2010–2018). Contact: stzafrir@univ.haifa.ac.il

https://doi.org/10.1515/9783110759808-011

Index

https://doi.org/10.1515/9783110759808-012